The Linux Companion

The Linux Companion

Everything you need to know to understand
and release the potential of Linux

Christopher Lynas

An imprint of **Pearson Education**

London · New York · Toronto · Sydney · Tokyo
Singapore · Madrid · Mexico City · Munich · Paris

PEARSON EDUCATION LIMITED

Head Office:
Edinburgh Gate
Harlow CM20 2JE
Tel: +44 (0)1279 623623
Fax: +44 (0)1279 431059

London Office:
128 Long Acre
London WC2E 9AN
Tel: +44 (0)20 7447 2000
Fax: +44 (0)20 7240 5771

First published in Great Britain 2000

© Pearson Education Limited 2000

The right of Christopher Lynas to be identified as Author of this Work has been asserted by him in
accordance with the Copyright, Designs and Patents Act 1988.

ISBN: 0-13-018321-0

British Library Cataloguing in Publication Data
A CIP catalogue record for this book can be obtained from the British Library

The programs in this book have been included for their instructional value. The publisher does not
offer any warranties or representation with respect to their fitness for a particular purpose,
nor does the publisher accept any liability for any loss or damage arising from their use.

Many of the designations used by manufacturers and sellers to distinguish their
product are claimed as trademarks. Pearson Education Limited has made every
attempt to supply trademark information about manufacturers and their products mentioned
in this book. A list of trademark designations and their owners appears on page xix.

10 9 8 7 6 5 4 3 2 1

Typeset by Pantek Arts Ltd, Maidstone, Kent
Printed and bound by Biddles Ltd, Guildford & King's Lynn.

The Publishers' policy is to use paper manufactured from sustainable forests.

This book is dedicated to my father:
DR EDWARD P. LYNAS
(1906–2000)

About the author

Christopher Lynas is a globally acknowledged Internet consultant and commentator. He has seen the Internet evolve at an astounding rate as a business tool. In this time he has also witnessed the growth and exponential development of Linux, each step of progress confirming his belief that it is the next big thing. He has challenged audiences from a wide range of industries in many countries to acknowledge the massive changes in their market sectors, due to these developments. How will we do business as the twenty-first century unfolds? What will we experience in our family and leisure time? He effectively bridges the gap between technology and the layperson, enlightening his audiences and encouraging them to study and respect the new and emerging technology.

With humour and finesse, he confronts his audiences with the truth of what they need to do, and how they need to think, to move into the future with success and optimism. Christopher Lynas is a sought-after speaker, dealing with how to adapt to the e-world society and the development of Linux.

He is a member of The Writers Guild and CimTech – The Chartered Institute of Marketing's Technology Interest Group.

Acknowledgements

First of all I would like to thank all at Pearson Education for the professional and dedicated manner they have shown in the publishing of this book.

My special thanks go the Pearson computing team: Acquisitions Editor, Clare Christian; Development Editor, Sally Carter; Senior Product Manager, Jonathan Hardy; and Senior Production Executive, Marilyn StClair. I am truly grateful to Katherin Ekstrom, Managing Editor, for her excellent work. Katherin Ekstrom has been a significant asset in this project. I would also like to thank Jane Hammett for expertly copy-editing this book.

I am honoured to have both Ruediger Berlich and Steve Menadue write the forewords for this book. Ruediger Berlich was a tremendus help in many of the technical aspects. Steve Menadue recognised the possibilities of Linux at an early stage when many had failed to understand and grasp its potential.

For taking time out of their busy schedules, I would like to express sincere thanks to: Alex Francis, Nick Davis, Jasmin U-Haque, Lenz Grimmer, Malcom Yates, Markus Rex, Michael Coyle, Manjit Saggu, Drew Crawford and Graeme Houston.

Sabine, my greatest gratitude and love is for you.

Contents

Foreword by IBM

An emerging technology at the crossroads – Linux

Not since the emergence of the Internet in the early 1990s has a technology generated such a buzz in computing circles. Many people are aware that it is an operating system for both desktops and servers that offers an alternative to Microsoft Windows. It is reputably stable and cost-effective. Most will be able to reel off the clichés: it is fast, it doesn't crash and it is free. But beyond that remains a great deal of confusion and hesitancy among business users.

Undoubtedly the emergence of Linux has caused great excitement among IT journalists and analysts, always eager to predict the next big thing in computing. However those who actually buy IT for business, or run a business dependent on IT, are, rightly, somewhat more circumspect. They will be asking why the great excitement. Why should Linux be considered as an alternative to Windows when they have already invested large sums of money into Windows-based systems that on the whole work. Why change now when 90% of the world uses Windows? After all, isn't Linux just a toy for nerds?

The truth is that Linux is now at a stage in its development where it does deserve serious consideration by business. For the first time in many years there is a credible alternative to Windows, certainly on the server side. It is hard however for business users to separate fact from fiction. Unfortunately, the IT industry isn't just about providing effective solutions to customers. Too often an operating system is seen as representing something that is either the right or the wrong way of doing things.

Talk to anyone involved in IT about Linux and you will soon find that emotions run high. One well-known US computer newspaper has an almost a weekly battle between two of its star columnists as to whether Linux is a good or bad thing which in turn generates furious debate among readers. This type of dialectic clouds the issue seriously, avoiding as it does the suitability of any operating system to business applications. In this sense it harms development of Linux and its applications. And it does little to assist those in business simply looking for cost-effective solutions.

The background to this book is of an emerging technology at the crossroads. Commercial Linux distributors such as Corel, SuSE and Red Hat are offering packages that are, now, easy to install with wider than ever hardware support.

Elsewhere, IBM and other vendors are able to offer complete Linux solutions in response to customer demand. At the same time the fact that they have off-the-shelf Linux solutions will lead other customers to consider this alternative. In a nutshell, it has entered the mainstream.

So those who have read much about Linux may already be at the point of deployment in at least some part of their infrastructure. In other words to perhaps give it a go.

As the business world turns increasingly to the Web and e-business, scalable, secure and robust server technologies are needed. This is one area where Linux has been successful with thousands of Web servers already running on Linux.

Chris Lynas looks at the history and development of Linux and the wider open source movement. After reading his work, you will be able to make up your own mind. You may wish to plunge in and start deploying Linux or you may feel that your business is not ready yet. In any case, you will certainly know more about Linux than you did before. You will discover that Linux does indeed have a lot to offer and is remarkably flexible. For example, deploying Linux, at least in some part of your infrastructure, could bring real benefits without abandoning legacy systems and investments.

Linux has moved from obscurity to the mainstream from the hacker's bench to a place on the servers of some of the largest companies in the world. It could now be your turn to investigate Linux and its potential.

Linux can no longer be dismissed as a flash in the pan. It is a serious operating system that deserves to take its place alongside Windows, in all its flavours, in a business world rapidly embracing the Internet. The presence of Linux gives us all new choices and new opportunities both as vendors and customers. We should welcome it, not as an ideology but as a new way of doing business.

Steve Menadue
Vice-President, Netfinity Servers, Europe, Middle East and Africa
IBM

Foreword by SuSE Linux

Being the managing director of SuSE Linux Ltd, the UK branch of Europe's leading manufacturer of Linux distributions, I am happy that this book has appeared.

Linux has come a long way since the first version was published by Linus Torvalds on the Internet in 1991. Today – nine years later – it has been adopted by software and hardware vendors as a widely used platform. Despite all prophecies of doom Linux features and stability have constantly improved over time and the underlying open source development model has proven to be effective. This has happened despite the fact that the speed of development has shifted to a higher gear due to the large-scale participation of commercial companies in the development of Linux. Open source development leads to convergence, not divergence.

It is fascinating to see how Linux has shaped the information technology market over time. While open source was not invented by Linux but had been common since the Free Software Foundation was founded by Richard Stallman in the 1980s, Linux has brought this development model to the public attention in a way unprecedented by other movements. Today open source has become a buzz-word. In 1991, however, it was crucial to make the source code available to other people and Linux with its multitude of applications would never have become as succesful as it is today without the help of thousands of people loosely connected via the Internet and email.

I started working with Linux in 1992 and at that time its main use was as a tool for students. This came about partially because the Internet was not as widely used as it is today and companies, such as SuSE, only just started to distribute the operating system (OS). So access to Linux was limited to people with Internet access. Today rarely a day goes by without some news about new big Linux startups and large companies, such as IBM, porting their software to Linux. Linux is widely used as the main OS, not only in the server market, but increasingly also on the desktop. Linux means business.

Linux has made the step from the specialist's OS to an OS that most people will find surprisingly easy to use and that can be used as the main, if not the only, OS on the desktop.

It is for this reason that I believe, Christopher Lynas' book is important, since it tries to make Linux in general, and SuSE Linux in particular, accessible and understandable for everyone.

Ruediger Berlich
SuSE Linux

Trademark Notice

Adobe Photoshop, Framemaker and PostScript are trademarks of Adobe Systems Incorporated; AIX, AS/400, DB2, PowerPC, RS/6000 and VisualAge are trademarks of Internationa;l Business machines Corporation; Amiga is a trademark of Commodore Business Machines; Atari is a trademark of the Atari Corporation; CorelDraw is a trademark of Corel Corporation; dBase is a trademark of Borland International Incorporated; Excite is a trademark of Excite Incorporated; Fortran and Oracle 8i/11i are trademarks of Oracle Corporation UK Ltd; Informix is a trademark of Informix Corporation; Internet Explorer, MS Excel, MS Powerpoint, MS Word, MS-DOS, VisualBasic, Windows, Windows 95, 98, NT, 3.1 are trademarks of Microsoft Corporation; JavaScript, NFS, Solaris, Sun and Sun Microsystems are trademarks of Sun Microsystems; Lotus Notes is a trademark of Lotus Development Corporation; Macintosh and MacOS trademarks of Apple Computer Incorporated; Netscape Navigator is a trademark of Netscape Communications Corporation; NetWare and Novell are trademarks of Novell Incorporated; Nintendo is a trademark of Nintendo of America Incorporated; OSF Motif is a trademark of Open Software Foundation; Pentium is a trademark of Intel Corporation; SAP is a trademark of SAP Aktiengesellschaft Systems, Applications and Products in Data Processing; Silicon Graphics is a trademark of Silicon Graphics Incorporated; SPARC is a trademark of 3Com Corporation; WordPerfect is a trademark of Sparo International Incorporated; WinModem is a trademark of WordPerfect Corporation; X Window System is a trademark of Massachusetts Institute of Technology; Yahoo! is a trademark of Yahoo Incorporated.

Introduction

Now this is not the end. It is not even the beginning of the end. But it is, perhaps, the end of the beginning.

Sir Winston Churchill 1874–1965

This epic began in Helsinki in 1991 where Linus Torvalds laid the foundations in creating an operating system for computers that would shape the evolution of civilisation in the twenty-first century. The origins of Linux resemble the beginning of what some consider the greatest masterpiece that the Internet has produced. Aided by thousands of enthusiastic programmers, this led to a meeting of minds that has now created a far more stable operating system than had previously existed.

The Internet has reinforced its position as the basis of the economy for the twenty-first century and will unquestionably become the most indispensable technology yet devised by the civilised world. It will change our economic systems as we proceed to a paperless society, taking advantage of online shopping, ease of communication and all the other benefits the Internet will bring us.

One of the reasons the Internet is such a global success is because there is not one person, company or government who controls it. As it evolves we shall see more government authorities *regulating* it but not controlling its evolution. Governments may wish to control it and software companies attempt to own and control as much of the Internet as they possibly can. It is in nobody's interest to have a monopoly controlling this transformation of our lives.

There are millions of minds and imaginations in the e-world population who have the intellectual capabilities and the programming skills to change the evolution of the e-world, and the thought of their future and their children's future being controlled by any one organisation or government is a clear motivation to them to achieve freedom from the shackles of 'closed' software. I believe that rich software companies in the twenty-first century will see their attempted control of the e-world decrease, as more and more individuals and companies adopt the more stable, reliable and open source software that Linux offers.

The e-world was not conceived in a software company's laboratory but in the world's universities and research institutions where unsung heroes influenced and created what we now know as the Internet. The Internet evolved from the world's best computer analysts and programmers. It evolved as everyone connected with it freely and openly shared his or her experiences to create a technology that could be shared by all.

The majority of today's computers run on 'closed' operating systems like DOS, Windows, or Macintosh, which means they are controlled by the company that created them. These companies are the only ones who can modify their software programs. Linux is the future; the open software aspect of its configuration allows any computer programmer to modify the inner workings of their computer just by using Linux as their operating system. The global support for Linux coupled with this capacity to change an operating system is set to change the whole concept of our e-world.

Linux is a phenomenon of the Internet. Born out of the project of a student it has grown to be more popular than any other freely available operating system. To many, Linux is a mystery. How can something that is free be important? It only reinstates the fact that the best things in life are free.

In a world dominated by a handful of large software corporations, how can something that has been written by a bunch of 'programmers' hope to compete? How can software contributed to by many different people in many different countries around the world have a hope of being stable and effective? Yet stable and effective it is and compete it does. Many universities and research establishments use it for their everyday computing needs. People run it on their home PCs and I would wager that most companies are using it somewhere even if they do not always realise that they do. Linux is used to browse the Web, host Web sites, write documents, send email and, as always with computers, to play games. Linux is definitely not a toy; it is a fully developed and professionally written operating system used by those who demand the highest standards all over the world.

The Linux concept is based on the fundamental principle that the best and most stable software comes from the global exchange of programming knowledge, where everyone is free to modify, develop, improve and then share the codes they have used. The global development of Linux is truly phenomenal in its extent and adaptation by thousands of supporters of open software. Linux is being developed, because of this combined global effort, at a momentous rate. If you visit any university's computer department or computer research institution you find the research is on Linux, not Windows or Macintosh systems. It is becoming more and more linked to the e-world.

We are about to see a technology shift of spectacular dimensions. I believe that Linux will affect the world economy and every computer-related industry in the world. The impact of Linux in the computing world will affect share prices, profits, margins and operating costs. Its effects will be immense, as this completely new and distinct software model takes control. How will this be? you may ask. The stability of the product and the economics of Linux, which is to all intents and purposes free, will ensure this. Consider the costs to a business of running a Windows NT program. This cost is negated by the adoption of Linux as the operating system. The managers of IT departments love the system. When accountants from finance departments realise the cost savings involved, they will adore it, because the cost of Linux is a fraction of that of competing technologies.

Companies will find it difficult to hold or even recruit the best staff in the programming world unless they are willing to accommodate their interest in Linux. Linux is more than an operating system, it really is a movement, with Linux being adopted by millions of serious computer developers around the world. Sony has recently announced that Linux will be the operating system that will run the next generation of interactive televisions. Linux will provide unprecedented business opportunities to those who take advantage of what it offers. It is the stability and economy of the system that will convince many that Linux is our future.

Linux and the open source movement have achieved such a global following that its impact on the future of the e-world will be unquestionable. If you want to understand the e-world of the future, get involved today to learn and appreciate what is going on.

In the early days of the e-world, software was complex and formidable. But the e-world gradually changed this, providing a technology that anyone could use and anyone could learn. Linux is emerging like the early days of the e-world. The potential of Linux is enormous; as you start to learn and understand it, it will grow on you. Visit all the Linux sites I mention in this book. Read and try to understand what it all means. I firmly believe that the future of the e-world will be found in Linux and the open source movement. As the twenty-first century unfolds, bringing with it changes in all our lives, we will come to realise that no one person or organisation should control these changes.

Most people use Linux as a simple tool, often just installing one of the many good CD-ROM-based distributions. A lot of Linux users use it to write applications or to run applications written by others. Many Linux users read the HOWTOs passionately and feel both the thrill of success when some part of the system has been correctly configured and the frustration of failure when it has not. A minority are bold enough to write device drivers and offer kernel patches to Linus Torvalds, the creator and maintainer of the Linux kernel. Linus accepts additions and modifications to the kernel sources from anyone, anywhere. This might sound like a recipe for chaos but Linus exercises strict quality control and merges all new code into the kernel himself.

The majority of Linux users do not look at how the operating system works, or how it fits together. This is a pity because looking at Linux is a very good way to learn more about how an operating system functions. Not only is it well written, all the sources are freely available for you to look at. This is because although the authors retain the copyright to their software, they allow the sources to be freely redistributable under the Free Software Foundation's GNU Public Licence.

I am not a 'techie' but have written this book from my own experience and the knowledge I have gained from Linux over the last three years when I realised the potential that Linux holds. There are many distributions of Linux and it can be difficult to choose a distribution when so many exist. In the main they are all excellent but which of these distributions is right for you? That will be your call, but I hope that after you have read this book you will be in a position to make a more informed judgement. I have experimented with many and always come back to SuSE. At home Linus Torvalds uses SuSE Linux as his Linux distribution on his computer and if it is good enough for him then it is most certainly good enough for me. SuSE Linux focuses on product excellence and this is reflected in its distribution. After spending some time with the SuSE development team in Nuremberg I soon came to realise that any product released by SuSE Linux which was anything but excellent would devalue their development ideals.

Linux is becoming easier to install and use. However, as with any operation of UNIX, there is often some massaging involved to get everything working correctly. This book has not been written as a technical how-to. In my writing, speaking and consultancy functions I do not focus on the technology but the implications of the technology. Technology today is impacting on everyone's lives in every direction and people are demanding to know the answers. This book does not make any assumptions about the knowledge or experience of the reader. I believe that interest in the subject matter will encourage self-education where necessary. That said, a degree of familiarity with computers, preferably PCs, will help the reader derive real benefit from the material. I am sure that anyone who reads this book will develop a much greater understanding of what SuSE Linux and Linux is all about, and I hope it will show you how great an operating system can be when you are working with raw computing power.

The more I use Linux, the more I become a Linux supporter. I appreciate that there are other operating systems but I prefer not to use them. Linux suits my needs perfectly. It is a superb, flexible and adaptable tool that will have major implications in all our lives.

What's in this book

I have split this book into eight chapters, each dealing with those issues which I believe will be of most importance, interest and relevance to readers of this book as we enter the twenty-first century.

1. Introducing Linux

2. Why Choose Linux?

3. Linux Applications and the Desktop

4. The Practicalities of Linux

5. Linux Fact and Fiction

6. The Business Aspect of SuSE

7. Linux Information and How to Find it

8. The Future of Linux

You will find in each chapter a wealth of information that will make you a more proficient and competent user of the resources and knowledge that awaits you in the e-world. Items of particular interest are highlighted in the text with the use of grey boxes. I am confident that you will find information that you never knew existed.

Systems used in this book

Throughout this book there are many references to sites on the World Wide Web. These will begin with either **www.** or **http://**, for example **http://eworldhandbook.com** or **www.eworldhandbook.com.**

These are the addresses you type in to reach the referenced site on the World Wide Web. All the WWW addresses listed were verified at the time of printing. However, since the Internet is constantly changing, some sites will change their addresses, move location or just disappear. Although we are unable to guarantee that all listings will remain in effect, updates and corrections will be available at the eWorld Handbook World Web Site at **www.eworldhandbook.com.**

Tell me about your experiences

To help improve future editions of this book your feedback is welcomed. Please let me have any suggestions or comments.

If you wish to share your online experiences with me, email me at the address below. Also, if you are aware of any small organisation that is developing any products or services for the Linux marketplace please let me know so that I can mention them in future editions.

I try to respond to all emails.

Christopher Lynas can be contacted at: **linux@eworldhandbook.com**.

Introducing Linux

This chapter introduces Linux. Many people have heard of Linux and want to understand what it is all about. This chapter will give you an understanding of Linux, although to fully understand its many facets and complexities is no easy task. I hope this book goes some way to showing you what a unique concept Linux is, and I hope you will find Linux as remarkable and fulfilling as I have.

Introducing Linux

Linux is a multi-user, multi-tasking freeware UNIX operating system, available for many platforms. PCs with x86 processors (Intel, AMD, Cyrix) from 386 onwards are the most commonly used platforms. Linux corresponds largely to the POSIX standard.

The name Linux is derived from the inventor of the system, Linus Torvalds. Strictly speaking, it only refers to the operating system kernel, but it is often used to describe the complete system, including the applications.

Linux today is made up of the following structures:

- *System software:* Whether you want to develop your own software or simply deploy a WWW server, an email/news server, an ISBN router or a file and application server, Linux provides you with all the necessary tools.

- *Applications:* A multitude of free software packages (some proven and used extensively, some still at an early beta-testing stage), complemented by a growing range of commercial software that is being ported on to this platform.

- *Development teams* all over the world, who continuously extend and improve Linux, making it available for new platforms.

- And last, hundreds of thousands of enthusiastic *users*, from students and interested individuals to large corporations such as the car rental company, Budget/Sikt, and IKEA, the Swedish furniture retailer with outlets all over the world, where business-critical applications are based on Linux.

The typical computer user buys a complete computer from a computer shop. Many computer users don't realise that when they buy a computer, they are actually buying two major items: the computer itself and the operating system which will operate it.

We know what the computer is: it's the box, the keyboard, the mouse and the monitor: in short, the computer is everything that can be seen or held. The computer is all of the sheet metal and the plastic, the circuits and the chips. To put it another way, the computer is the physical set of components which can be put in a box and carried home.

Most users, however, do not have a clear understanding of the operating system. The operating system is the set of actions and information displayed by the computer. The operating system determines what the computer does once it is switched on: the text, the graphics, the applications, and even the Internet access. The operating system determines what is shown on the screen, how files will be saved to disk, and what will come out of the printer. The next section will go into this in more detail.

What is an operating system?

An operating system is a group of programs that help you operate your computer. It could be considered the administration of your computer's internal society, the central program that tells the other programs what they may do and provides services they need. A computer might contain more than one operating system, but only one operating system may be in command at any one time. The action of starting or loading the operating system is called *booting* the computer.

Windows 95/98 is an example of

an operating system. MS-DOS is (or was) also an operating system. Linux is an operating system as well. All of these systems perform similar tasks.

An operating system normally consists of some basic components. A *kernel*, a core program that controls the essential hardware (the processor and memory, for example); some *device drivers* that control other system hardware (network cards, soundcards); and a *shell*, a program that communicates with the user and allows the user to manipulate the computer.

The shell is the only part of the operating system that a normal computer user will see. Each operating system shell presents a different *user interface* or operating environment. An Apple computer running MacOS will look different to a PC running Windows 95 or Linux, and the way the user goes about accomplishing tasks and giving instructions to the computer is also different. MS-DOS requires you to type commands at a text prompt to start programs, while in MacOS you must use the mouse to click on a picture to perform the same task.

The operating system acts as a type of translator; a human user doesn't know how to speak binary machine language. The operating system allows the user to receive communication from the computer via the screen and the printer, and to send communication to the computer via the keyboard or disk drive(s). The operating system also tells various components of the computer, like the screen, the printer, the disk drive(s), and programs, such as your favourite games, how to talk to each other effectively.

Without an operating system, a computer is merely a mass of raw materials which can be switched on, but which will not do anything useful. The operating system which nearly every computer buyer receives with a new computer is Microsoft Windows. This operating system, more commonly called simply 'Windows', is not a part of the computer at all. Windows is simply one operating system among a whole host of others, which can be used with PCs.

Linux in the context of operating systems

Linux is a new way for your computer to behave. It is a new set of pictures, screens, menus and instructions for the various chips and circuits of your computer to manipulate and for you, the user, to interact with. Linux can be installed on your computer instead of Windows or MacOS, and Linux provides many of the same tools: Linux can talk to a printer, save a file to your hard disk, or display a picture on your screen. Users can type letters using Linux, browse the Web using Linux, or edit a company spreadsheet while using Linux, in much the same way that these tasks are accomplished while using Windows or MacOS.

Linux should not simply be regarded as a direct replacement for the operating system which came with your computer, however. It is not simply a 'better' Windows or MacOS, though in many ways it can be superior. Instead, Linux should be considered simply as a different operating system, a new set of habits, thoughts and tools for you and your computer to share. More importantly, because Linux fundamentally affects the operation of your computer, it can never be a 'plug-in replacement' for the operating system, which came with your computer. Your favourite Windows games will not easily work in Linux, nor will many of your favourite tools, such as Microsoft Office or Internet Explorer. On the other hand, Linux has games and many powerful tools of its own, such as StarOffice and Netscape Communicator, which perform similarly to Microsoft Office and Internet Explorer.

Who is responsible for Linux?

Now that you know what Linux is, and you realise that other operating systems, like Windows and MacOS, are maintained by Microsoft and Apple respectively, you're probably wondering which company is responsible for Linux.

Surprisingly, Linux is unlike Windows or MacOS in this respect. Linux is not maintained or owned by any single company or for-profit organisation. Linux was started as a learning project by a computer science student in Finland named Linus Torvalds (hence the name Linux). Linus was motivated by two factors when he created Linux. First, he wanted to learn more about the microprocessor he was studying at the time – and what better way to learn than by creating an operating system to talk to it? Second, Linus wanted to have access to a mature family of operating systems known as UNIX systems, which are often found on very large computers. UNIX operating systems were expensive at the time, because they didn't work on personal computers, only large mainframes. So, Linus set out to make something that worked and looked like a UNIX operating system, but which would run on a personal computer. And he succeeded.

He began the Linux experiment nearly a decade ago and has since graduated, but he is still in charge of the Linux core today, though many companies now exist to help promote and distribute the Linux operating system. Millions of computer science students worldwide use Linux daily for their calculations and studies, and many people help Linus to maintain Linux, release new versions, and keep it all developing at an impressive rate.

How computer programs are made

A computer program is a list of instructions given to a computer to make it perform a specific task or series of tasks. Computers do not understand English, so programmers must communicate these instructions to the computer in a language the computer understands. Computers, however, can only operate in numbers, which makes a computer's language very difficult for humans to understand.

The solution to this problem is to create an intermediate language that both humans and computers can understand. This is called programming language, and currently there are several different languages. Programmers create a list of instructions for the computer in a programming language such as C, Pascal or Fortran. This list of instructions is known as *source code*. It is textual in nature, and readable to humans (who speak the language). Programmers do all their work in this source code, changing instructions to fix bugs, add features, or alter the appearance of a program.

When a programmer believes he has perfected the instructions for his program, he uses a special program called a *compiler* to translate his human-readable text instructions into computer-readable numbers that correspond to the same instructions. The resulting file is usable by computers but incomprehensible to humans. This is called *object code*. The resulting executable file is often called *binary*, after the number system used by the computer. This translation from source code into binary object code is a one-way process. It is impossible to translate a binary executable back into the original source code.

The binary executable is what you need if you want to run and use a program. This is what you will usually receive when you purchase shrink-wrapped software from a retail store. The source code is what you need if you want to understand how a program works internally, or if you want to change, add to or improve a program. If you have the source code and an appropriate compiler, you can produce the binary executable, but this does not work in reverse.

A brief history of Linux

The goal for most programmers is to create a stable and reliable program or application that will earn the respect of their peers. Linus Torvalds went much further, laying down the foundation that personifies the ultimate hack.

Linux began in 1991 as a typical programming bit of fun, written to run on a PC with 4 Mb of RAM as a free version of the costly commercial UNIX operating system. Today, Linux has an installed base conserva- tively estimated at around 14 million users. And they're not just spotty adolescents playing in their bed- rooms: Linux vendors say that most of the top companies in the USA have bought Linux in some form. Linux's installed base may not be on the level of Windows, but Linux has made its mark in just half the time that Microsoft has been around. Microsoft gives you Windows – Linux gives you the complete house.

Linux is freely distributable – one CD-ROM can be passed on hundreds of times – so it's particularly popular in countries just getting wired to the Internet. And technologically, Linux eclipses all the other brands of UNIX. Linux is far and above the most vital part of the UNIX market. Dennis Ritchie, one of the two fathers of the original UNIX, calls Linux 'commendable'.

The saga of Linux has many strands. It is the story of Linus. It is also the story of the Internet as a model for distributed collaboration. Indeed, Linux has used the Internet as a medium to create a huge patchwork of code that defines a rapidly growing e-world, the tightly linked community of those who make and use it. What unites these programmers is the drive to

Did you know that...?

UNIX

UNIX is an operating system widely used on workstations. UNIX supports vital concepts, such as running different machines on a network. It consists of a kernel, a shell and applications. Since the mid-1990s, there has been a freeware version available for PCs, – Linux.

Did you know that...?

CD-ROM drive

There are various types of CD-ROM drive. The most common type is ATAPI drives, which are connected to a (E)IDE hard disk controller. There are also SCSI CD-ROM drives, which are operated via a SCSI host adapter, CD-ROM drives connected to the parallel port and proprietary CD-ROM drives which are controlled via special controller cards or via the soundcard. Proprietary drives also need special drivers.

create the world's greatest operating system (OS), one more powerful than any commercial UNIX, able to run on practically any hardware, and infinitely customisable. An OS that is fully the equal of Microsoft's flagship, Windows NT – with true multi-tasking, virtual memory, shared libraries, TCP/IP networking and other advanced features.

Many see Linux as NT's most serious competitor, the only practical alternative to the Microsoft monoculture – singular proof of the ideal that says we should have a choice.

Linux, it turns out, was no intentional masterstroke, but an incremental process, a combination of experiments, ideas and tiny scraps of code that gradually evolved into an organic whole. Many of Linus's formative years of low-level programming were spent poring over a Sinclair QL launched in 1984 that had many faults but one real virtue: it was a true multi-tasking system that allowed advanced hacking. But the key event that ultimately led to Linux occurred in the autumn of 1990, when Linus took a UNIX course at the University of Helsinki, where he studied and eventually earned a master's degree in computer science.

Linus began to experiment, using Minix as scaffolding to develop a new program. He says he never intended to create a kernel, the part of an operating system where the real processing and control work is done. Instead, a purely practical need to read UseNet newsgroups drove him to modify those first two processes. 'At some point,' he recalls, 'I just noticed, hey, I almost have this functionality.'

In 1991 he needed a simple terminal emulation program to access newsgroups. So Linus sat down and wrote one – based on his two-process lash-up. As Linus tells it, doing so was simply a matter of changing those As and Bs into something else. 'One process is reading from the keyboard and sending to the modem' – which then connects to the university computer – 'and the other is reading from the modem' – receiving the newsfeed – 'and sending to the screen.'

But there was something else Linus needed: drivers. A driver acts as a software buffer between something central (like the kernel) and something peripheral (like a keyboard, screen or modem). It could be built straight into the kernel, but then it would be necessary to rewrite the kernel each time you wanted to use a bigger screen, a different keyboard or a faster modem.

In the summer of 1991 – just six months after he got his first PC – Linus found he needed to download some files. But before he could read and write to a disk, he recalls, 'I had to write a disk driver. Then I had to write a file system so I could read the Minix file system in order to be able to write files and read files to upload them. When you have task-switching, a file system and device drivers, that's UNIX' – or at least its kernel. Linux was born.

This fledgling system would have been short-lived had Linus not mentioned it in the Minix newsgroup. His early posting prompted an offer of space on an FTP server at the Helsinki University of Technology, letting people download the first public version of Linux.

By January 1992, only around 100 people were using Linux, but they provided a critical online baptism. Those early uploads and comments were crucial. Particularly important were the patches sent in by fellow programmers to fix problems they found with the code. Anybody anywhere on the Net could obtain the basic Linux files. Email enabled them to comment and offer improvements, while UseNet provided a forum for discussion.

A kernel on its own is not much use, even if it is being refined constantly through patches sent by interested programmers. Part of the reason Linux took off so spectacularly is that nearly everything else needed for a complete OS was already there. These programs-in-waiting were part of the Free Software Foundation's GNU project. The recursively named effort – 'What's GNU? GNU's Not UNIX' – was begun in 1984 by Richard Stallman as a reaction against some of the draconian rules imposed by vendors on software users.

GNU's aim was to write a complete 'free' version of UNIX – the kernel and all the associated elements – that is, one that gave users the freedom to share and change software but not add restrictions and impose them on others. With the Linux kernel, Stallman says, 'the available free software added up to a complete system.'

Rather than wait for someone to write applications designed specifically for his operating system, Linus tweaked Linux to perfectly fit GNU's pre-existing applications. 'I never ported programs,' Linus says. 'I ported the kernel to work with the programs. Linux was never the primary reason for anything – user programs have always been the reason.'

A similarly sensible approach allowed Linux to acquire, almost overnight, a graphical user interface (GUI) similar to Windows – this was indispensable for its wider acceptance. (Until then, Linux was controlled through obscure commands entered as text at a prompt, rather like DOS.) The GUI was provided by the Xfree86 project, a non-profit group that provides free software for PC versions of the X Window system.

Linus also adopted the standard GNU licensing scheme called *copyleft*. The general public licence, or GPL, allows users to sell, copy and change copylefted programs – which can also be copyrighted – but you must pass along the same freedom to sell or copy your modifications and change them further. You must also make the source code of your modifications freely available.

GPL has proved a powerful force for Linux's success. First, it has encouraged a flourishing commercial Linux sector. GPL also has given programmers an additional incentive to join in the essentially philanthropic spirit of the Linux movement. The licence has ensured that their work is freely distributable, but not unfairly exploited or locked into proprietary products by unscrupulous commercial organisations.

In a sense, GPL provided a written constitution for the new online movement of Linux programmers. The licence said it was acceptable to build on, or incorporate wholesale, other people's code – just as Linux did – and even to make money doing so (programmers have to eat, after all). But the programmer's fundamental law of software must not be broken: source code must be freely available for further hacking.

In March 1994, the official Linux version 1.0 appeared, almost as a formal declaration of independence. By then the user base was already large, and the core Linux development team substantial. Among the thousands of files Linux contains, there is one called simply Credits. In it are the names, addresses and contributions of the main Linux programmers. The list runs to more than 100 names, scattered around the world.

The growth of the development team reflected the natural development of Linux itself. Linus began choosing and relying on a few trusted lieutenants from whom he would take larger trusted patches.

The Linux approach is deceptively simple. All programmers are free to work on any additional features or improvements. Even in the earliest stages, new code is freely downloadable for users to try and critique: beta testing is not a last-minute attempt to catch the worst flaws, but an integral part of the process. When several people work on the same area, they may compete or combine; if they compete, the best code surfaces through raw and thorough selection.

This freewheeling situation has allowed hundreds of thousands of users to employ Linux on perhaps tens of thousands of hardware configurations: Linux supports everything from an Intel 386 to a Pentium Pro, along with platforms based on Alpha (Digital's RISC chip), SPARC (Sun's RISC chip), MIPS (port to Silicon Graphics' RISC chip under development), and MkLinux (a version of Linux that runs on Intel and PowerPC machines). Users also have, via the Net, ready means for communicating any problems to the person who knows the program best – the author. That can be a big plus, or a distinct minus. While serious programmers might like having a tête-à-tête with another programmer, most regular users just want their questions answered fast. Providing a reliable Linux helpdesk could help a commercial vendor bring Linux to the masses.

The automatic selection of programmers to work in the areas they know best, and the ability of the system to expand endlessly by delegating tasks in this naturally distributive way, has produced other benefits. Linux has rapidly obtained features that have taken commercial vendors many years to develop.

Indeed, the pace of upgrades is astounding: from the earliest days, the latest patches typically appeared every week. And yet in parallel, there is always a stable release distribution that moves forward just as inexorably when the new features have been thoroughly tested. Linux generally proceeds with point releases – 1.1, 1.2, and so on. There is also a complicated system of subpoint releases such as 1.1.12. When a big enough jump in software functionality occurs, developers move to the next version, a process normally presided over by Linus.

This two-track development process has made Linux probably more advanced and yet more stable than any other version of UNIX today. Linux is now entering an era of pure development instead of just catching up, and this is where its huge number of developers and testers will give it an incredible edge over any other operating system – NT included.

The latest version of Linux offers 64-bit processing (NT and many UNIX systems are only 32-bit); symmetric multi-processing, which allows the simultaneous deployment of several chips in a system; and networking more advanced than that of any other operating system.

A related advantage of Linux's developmental structure is that security fixes typically turn up faster than from commercial suppliers. For example, when a 'Ping of Death' assault of multiple, low-level messages crashed several operating systems worldwide, a quick patch to Linux enabled the attack to be thwarted in a couple of hours. Users of other operating systems had to wait far longer for their systems to be fixed.

Did you know that...?

System administrator

This is the person responsible for maintaining and supervising a complex system or network. Generally, the system administrator is the only person who has access to all parts of the system (root permissions).

Open Source

One of the first things which happened to change the face of software was the release of the Netscape browser's source code. This brought to public attention a conflict between two dramatically different and fundamentally opposed styles of software development, a confrontation that had been in the making for 30 years but became inevitable after the advent of the World Wide Web and the explosion of the Internet's popularity in 1993–1994.

The first of the two programming styles is *closed source*, the traditional factory-production model of proprietary software, in which customers get a sealed block of bits that they cannot examine, modify or evolve. Microsoft is the most famous practitioner of this approach. The other style is *open source*, the Internet engineering tradition in which source code is generally available for inspection, independent peer review and rapid evolution. The standard-bearer of this approach is the Linux operating system.

The open source model threatens to make closed source software obsolete. To understand why, we need to step back from Microsoft and Linux and consider that engineers and some high-tech executives are attracted to open source development for three reasons: reliability, reduced cost of ownership and improved strategic business risk.

Historically, the way engineers and scientists have ensured high reliability of their products is through peer review. Physicists don't conceal their experimental plans from each other; instead, they check and recheck each other's work. Engineers don't build dams or suspension bridges without having other engineers independent of the original design group examine the blueprints.

Software companies do not generally do peer review of their code. And in the software industry, reliability has always been poor. Crashes, hangs and lost data are still commonplace. These observations may seem unrelated, but the connection is clear when you look at the infrastructure of the Internet.

Most of the software that runs the Internet, like Apache (the most common Web server), Perl programming language and Sendmail email system was developed under the open source model, and its reliability is extremely high. This level of reliability is even more significant given that the Internet is multiplatform, heterogeneous and international and has remained backward-compatible through 30 years and several generations of technology.

A simple and compelling pattern is starting to emerge. Open source software goes through rigorous peer review and has high reliability. Without peer review, software reliability suffers. This fact in itself may be sufficient to marginalise closed source commercial development.

Total cost of ownership is also drastically affected by open source software. In a closed source world, a producer charges for the bits and has an effective monopoly on service for its products. Accordingly, major closed source packages cost thousands of pounds up front, plus thousands of pounds a year in service and upgrade costs. In the open source world, by contrast, the bits are free, the source code is available and the provider doesn't have a lock on the service and upgrade business. Accordingly, both initial and annual costs are low.

But the most important long-term effect of open source software will be on strategic business risk. To see why, think again about the supplier's monopoly with closed source software. The chief information officer (CIO) of any company typically spends vast amounts of money on a strategic business system with software that no one in the company can modify. And that CIO must depend on a single vendor to service the new system. Thus, changes to those systems serve only the business plans of the vendors, rather than the companies who buy from them.

When companies use Windows operating systems, Microsoft is the only choice they have for service because only Microsoft has access to Windows source code. If a company chooses a Linux distribution then they have the support of that company and 100,000 Internet developers who will cheerfully assist using the same free, common and exhaustively debugged code base.

Open source software is the best recipe for high reliability, dramatically lowers total cost of ownership and effectively puts the software customer in the driver's seat. With these factors at work, it may not be long before buying closed source software is considered financially irresponsible.

Software that is available only in binary executable format is *proprietary software*. Software that is available in source code format is *open software*. If it meets certain criteria it may also be certified as open source. Check out **www.opensource.org/osd.html** (Figure 1.1).

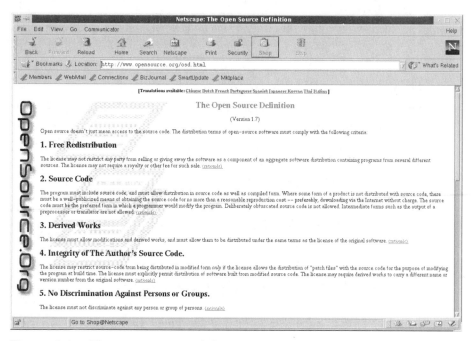

Figure 1.1   The open source definition

The Open Source Definition (Version 1.7)

'Open source' doesn't just mean that you can gain access to the source code. The distribution terms of open source software must comply with the following criteria (as shown in Figure 1.1):

1. **Free Redistribution**

    The license may not restrict any party from selling or giving away the software as a component of an aggregate software distribution containing programs from several different sources. The license may not require a royalty or other fee for such sale.

2. **Source Code**

    The program must include source code, and must allow distribution in source code as well as compiled form. Where some form of a product is not distributed with source code, there must be a well-publicized means of obtaining the source code for no more than a reasonable reproduction cost – preferably, downloading via the Internet without charge. The source code must be the preferred form in which a programmer would modify the program. Deliberately obfuscated source code is not allowed. Intermediate forms such as the output of a pre-processor or translator are not allowed.

3. **Derived Works**

    The license must allow modifications and derived works, and must allow them to be distributed under the same terms as the license of the original software.

4. **Integrity of The Author's Source Code**

    The license may restrict source code from being distributed in modified form *only* if the license allows the distribution of 'patch files' with the source code for the purpose of modifying the program at build time. The license must explicitly permit distribution of software built from modified source code. The license may require derived works to carry a different name or version number from the original software.

5. **No Discrimination Against Persons or Groups**

    The license must not discriminate against any person or group of persons.

6. **No Discrimination Against Fields of Endeavor**

    The license must not restrict anyone from making use of the program in a specific field of endeavor. For example, it may not restrict the program from being used in a business, or from being used for genetic research.

7. **Distribution of License**

   The rights attached to the program must apply to all to whom the program is redistributed without the need for execution of an additional license by those parties.

8. **License Must Not Be Specific to a Product**

   The rights attached to the program must not depend on the program's being part of a particular software distribution. If the program is extracted from that distribution and used or distributed within the terms of the program's license, all parties to whom the program is redistributed should have the same rights as those that are granted in conjunction with the original software distribution.

9. **License Must Not Contaminate Other Software**

   The license must not place restrictions on other software that is distributed along with the licensed software. For example, the license must not insist that all other programs distributed on the same medium must be open source software.

2

Why Choose Linux?

Features of Linux

One remarkable feature of Linux is its price: the system, as such, is free, and can be copied and distributes without restriction. Appropriately prepared versions, such as SuSE Linux, can be purchased inexpensively. The biggest advantage of Linux is the free availability of its source code.

Existing systems often cause exasperated developers to say 'We will just have to live with that.' Linux enables them to say, 'We will have to change that!' When a bug becomes known, a patch to fit is often available within days. The last years have reinforced just how important this is. It is entirely down to this unlimited access to the source code that such a large number of interested, competent and expert users all over the world contribute actively to the further development of Linux, bringing it to the level at which it stands today.

This freedom also means that users are not tied to one supplier when it comes to service and support. On the contrary, they can pick the best and most appropriate company on the market for them in terms of price and expertise.

Extensive Linux environments such as SuSE Linux open up the advantages of Linux to a broader audience. SuSE Linux has been prepared in such a way that even inexperienced users and newcomers to UNIX can cope with the installation. In addition, the package contains many extra utilities, programs and demos. SuSE Linux also provides an extensive manual, which should provide the answers to all queries, whether from novices or experienced users. And, as a special service, SuSE Linux provides every customer with a free 60-day installation support by fax or email. To conclude this section, Linux is designed to be fast, responsive and flexible. There is excellent and free Internet support and documentation available. The graphical user interface is similar in design to that on any other system and a very powerful command line alternative is also available.

Why should you adopt Linux?

You've heard about Linux, and seen lots of the hype: Linux IPOs are setting records on stock markets all over the world, and Linus Torvalds is becoming a household name. You may also know that Linux is growing faster than Windows in the server space. It's cropping up more and more on the desktop as well, although the general consensus is that Linux is not yet ready to mount a serious challenge to Windows there.

But we're starting to see Linux for sale more often, and in more places. Just look around any bookshop and you will discover that Linux has more titles on the shelves than Windows. This might cause you to start thinking about Linux. Something is happening here that you don't understand, and you're afraid it's about to pass you by.

Windows is not going to go away any time soon, and neither are Macs. Both will be around for years and years. Let's go back to the original question – why should you adopt Linux?

One of the most common answers to the question is that Linux is more stable than Windows. That is especially true of consumer versions of Windows, like Windows 95 and 98. But Linux is also more stable than Windows NT, often measuring periods of uptime in months instead of weeks (like NT) or days (like Windows 9x).

How important is this increased stability? That depends on you. If you use your computer to play games, surf the Net and exchange email, it may not be as critical as it is to someone who is running an application around the clock, using the computer in a small business or doing important research. But it often only takes a single system crash, with the inevitable loss of documents that goes along with it, to motivate even casual users to seek more stability.

You might also want to switch because Linux can extract more performance from your existing hardware. Older machines with less memory and less powerful central processing units (CPUs) can boost performance nicely by changing from Windows to Linux. Raw speed is important in game play, number crunching, image processing, database management and software compilation. After spending years buying more powerful hardware in order to keep pace with the memory hogging and speed loss that is inherent in Windows applications, it's a relief to find an operating system that helps performance instead of hurting it.

People also list file systems as another reason for making the change. I don't agree with this one, unless we're talking about the number of file systems supported by Linux versus the number supported by Windows. If you work in an environment with a lot of different platforms, the fact that Linux supports a lot of file systems while Windows supports only a few can be very important.

Perhaps this year Linux will have a journaling file system in place, which will justify the move all by itself. A journaling file system uses an intent log, or journal. Before metadata changes are actually performed, they are logged to a separate journal. The operation is then performed. If the system crashes during the operation, there is enough information in the log to 'replay' the log record and complete the operation. This approach does not require a full scan of the file system, thus it yields very quick runs on large file systems – generally a few seconds for a mulitple-gigabyte file system. In addition, because all information for the pending operation is saved, no removals or lost-and-found moves are required.

Money is another motivation to adopt Linux. But perhaps your reason is less concrete. Perhaps you want to expand your knowledge of internals and drivers and applications, which you cannot do with Windows. In the Windows world, you can buy books that teach you about drivers and internals, but you're only going to get as close to the underlying code as Microsoft allows. You can buy thousands of applications, but you're never going to see their source code or how they accomplish the things they do. You're never going to find a bug and contribute a fix.

Unless you sign your life away in a nuclear bombproof non-disclosure agreement, you're never going to see the Windows source code either. Before Windows 95 was released, Microsoft not only required that the engineers who had worked on the system sign such an agreement, but also demanded that they did not develop applications for other operating systems for three years. Microsoft only withdrew this requirement after very serious protests from the developer community.

With Linux, you have the operating system and you have the source code for it. You can configure the kernel so that it matches your particular hardware set-up, or even delve into the code and create a customised kernel. Everything is right there in front of you. The same is true of thousands of open source utilities and applications. This is better than just having a book; this is the real thing. Of course, there are plenty of books as well, if you want to read them.

There are many other reasons for deciding to use Linux. Freedom is the reason that Linus wrote Linux in the first place, and freedom is the reason he chose the GPL to protect it. He wanted Linux always to be available, and free, for those who came after him. You lose freedom as a Windows user, whether you realise it or not. In its place, you're given shrink-wrapped licensing terms that Microsoft can change on a whim. Even though you can choose not to accept unwanted Windows software under the terms of your end-user licensing agreement, very few OEMs (original equipment manufacturers) honour that agreement in practice and refund the cost of the OS.

Here's another example. If you bought a Windows NT workstation and intended to use it to host a Web site, you found that your freedom to do so evaporated the moment Microsoft changed its licensing terms. Faced with competition from Netscape, Microsoft decided that its users were no longer free to have more than ten simultaneous connections to an NT workstation. In a wink of a Microsoft lawyer's eye, your rights to use the software for the purpose for which you purchased it in the first place disappeared.

The reason for this change was not technical, despite company claims; it was predatory. Microsoft forced its own customers to buy a Windows NT server, the cost of which is more than double that of an NT workstation. By doing so, the company drove users toward its own Web server software, which comes bundled 'free' with NT server.

Why I Use SuSE Linux

I discovered Linux over three years ago. I honestly don't remember where I heard of it, but I remember thinking it was a great idea. Software written by people from all over the world, provided absolutely free, with source code freely available. As long as there are users there will be bug fixes, because anyone can tinker with it. And it was based on UNIX, the most successful, most powerful operating system in the world.

So my primary reason for switching to Linux was to have an OS and software that I can get for a low cost, upgrade for a low cost, and not have to worry about it crashing. It works because it has been tested and improved by thousands of people who use the program and have the resources to correct it. Higher quality and lower price appealed to the Scotsman in me.

My other reason for switching is Microsoft. Please do not misunderstand: me: I am not a Microsoft basher. Nor am I a Microsoft lover. It has simply been, until now, a one-horse race in the desktop operating system market. A situation that the courts are investigating today.

What other company makes an operating system, or a user environment, for PCs? No offence meant to Apple Mac, but the Mac is not competition for Microsoft and Microsoft now owns a piece of Apple.

But Linux is something that Microsoft can't compete with. It's free, it's open source, it's a workstation OS and a server OS. It's portable to all kinds of hardware; end-user support and documentation are available for free all over the Internet, and commercial vendors can provide priority support to corporate customers. If the corporate users are unhappy with the support they get they can switch to another vendor, but they do not have to switch software.

I really believe that Linux will soon be the OS to beat, with Microsoft running in second place. Linux is already gaining market share in the world of Internet servers, and new efforts are being made in Linux communities to make Linux a viable desktop solution for 'normal' users; in other words, a replacement for Windows 95/98/2000.

Is SuSE Linux ready for desktop use in the home and office marketplace? When I was in Nuremberg in January I noticed that many of the SuSE employees were employed in administrative positions. About half of SuSE's 350 employees are non-technical. There are employees of every kind – from secretaries to accountants. SuSE's employees use SuSE Linux as their only operating system. New non-technical employees usually get used to the way SuSE Linux works within a very short time. If they couldn't perform their daily work efficiently and without problems, SuSE would be out of business within a few weeks. The mere fact that SuSE has developed, in a very short period of time, into a global company, with an infrastructure running solely on SuSE Linux, is proof that SuSE Linux is a viable solution for the desktop.

Many people experienced difficulties in installing Linux in the past, but it is getting easier to install and SuSE Linux latest release is the easiest yet. This relese features more improvements to SuSE's graphical installation tool, YaST2, **www.suse.co/Product/yast2.html** (see Figure 2.1), including the automatic detection of more hardware and a simplified configuration of Internet connection, soundcard, network and printer. Automatic detection and configuration means that the system automatically recognises and runs your soundcard, printer, mouse, and other peripherals right from the start, so that you do not have to identify them individually to the system.

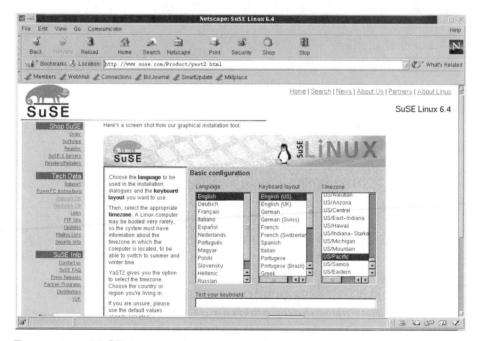

Figure 2.1   YaST2, Linux graphical installation tool

Having said that, there are still a few areas where Linux is lagging behind. Most notably, new drivers for hardware are not developed by the hardware manufacturer themselves, but usually by the Linux community. Also, unlike with Windows, ISPs do not usually distribute Linux connectivity kits that provide an out-of-the-box Internet set-up. Linux distributors such as SuSE work around that problem by providing their own (generic) set-up. These issues are, however, related more to the configuration and installation of the system. It is my firm belief that SuSE Linux has come to the point in its development where users whatever their knowledge level can use and enjoy the SuSE Linux system.

Linux compared to other operating systems

Why should I use Linux instead of Windows or MacOS?

There are a number of situations in which Linux will outperform other operating systems such as Windows or MacOS. You might want to try Linux if:

- **You handle large amounts of information**
  With an incredibly fast native file system, powerful database engines available at no cost with source code included, the ability to reduce thousands of mouse-clicks to single command lines, support for high-performance configurations and a networked distributed core designed for data processing automation across the network, Linux is the master of data storage, retrieval, manipulation and sharing.

- **You can't afford the software you need**
  Linux itself is a free operating system – it has no licensing fees, whether per user, per copy, or per use. But even more importantly, nearly every piece of Linux software is available without charge. Powerful Web servers such as Apache, the most widely used server on the Internet, SQL engines, typesetting engines, scientific data acquisition systems and even research-oriented clustering tools are all free for Linux users, even for commercial use. No program for Linux has ever started free and then later become a proprietary or pay-per-licence product.

- **Performance is of key importance**
  At its core, Linux enjoys better scalability, quicker interrupt latency and more advanced memory management than any other workstation or PC-class operating system. And with built-in or free support for symmetric

multi-processing (up to 16 processors), software RAID (levels zero through five) and workstation clustering, Linux's performance is unbeatable at any cost.

- **You need a truly stable computing platform**
  Linux is stable. There can be no simpler statement about an operating system, and yet, in today's computing industry, the ability to make such a statement is nothing short of miraculous. No 'blue screen of death', no resets, no lockups. Uptimes (time without reboot) are counted in months or years, not days or hours, no matter how heavy your network traffic or input/output loads.

- **Your network must remain secure**
  Linux is based on UNIX-like systems and, because of this, enjoyed from the beginning one of the most mature security-oriented code bases and philosophies in the computing industry. Furthermore, you have access to every piece of code in the system. If you manage to find a hole, you can fix it yourself in five minutes. And there are millions of Linux users world-wide who step in to fix new security holes in just this manner – usually within hours of the problem's discovery. You get a rapid fix for your problem, and for free, without ever having to call support or install a costly update.

> ### Did you know that...?
>
> **Network**
> A network is a functional connection between different computers. There are different types of topologies, depending on how the machines are connected, such as ring, star, bus and tree. Some well-known hardware standards for networks are Ethernet, Token Ring and ISDN. TCP, UDP and IPX (acting on different layers) are some typical networking software protocols.

- **Your network is a multi-platform nightmare**
  Linux includes native support for networks by Microsoft, Novell, Apple and others, including UNIX vendors such as Sun, Compaq and Hewlett-Packard. Without expensive software or hardware, a single ultra-stable Linux file server can talk to all of the users in your office, regardless of which type of computer or network you have.

- **You would like the same operating system for all of your computers**
  You have an office which is 50 per cent PC, 40 per cent Mac, and then there are those two Amiga computers upstairs, the Sun/SPARC department in the basement and a whole army of Silicon Graphics workstations in the other building. You could keep the manuals and training sessions for each operating platform, or you could just install Linux on all of them, and train workers for one operating system: Linux.

■ You need a powerful multi-user solution

There still exists no better multi-user solution than UNIX. Users who have never experienced UNIX-style user and workgroup management simply cannot comprehend the security and flexibility of the UNIX multi-user paradigm. In Linux, each user owns his or her own files, environment and even an 'instance' of the graphical desktop; indeed, Linux allows for a single machine to manage graphical desktops and file systems for multiple users or groups simultaneously and across the network, without the need for 'thin clients' or 'network computers,' all transparently, and all without compromising security.

■ You need a UNIX computer

Linux is a fully-fledged UNIX-like operating system, which is POSIX-compliant, and may even be branded with the official UNIX name by the open group at some point in the future. Unlike more costly UNIX solutions, however, Linux servers can often be assembled for mere hundreds of pounds.

■ You're a developer or computer science student

How many languages can you name? C, C++, Forth, Fortran, Ada, Lisp, Python, Perl, Tcl/Tk, BASIC, Java – the list goes on and on. Install Linux and start compiling in the language of your choice, almost always for free, and always with access to excellent UNIX-world development tools. And how would you like native Java binary support? Start your Java application from the command line, instead of having to work within an awkward browser.

Linux distributions

Why are there so many different kinds of Linux?

Since there is no official, central version of Linux, each distribution maintainer is free to construct an operating system which suits their own goals and/or market research. Though the most important aspects of operation remain similar across all distributions of Linux, different distributions will include or emphasise different applications or different behaviours.

The more familiar operating systems such as Windows or MacOS provide for a very basic, consistent level of functionality on a single type of machine. Because Linux serves a much broader community, Linux must remain more flexible. Different Linux users perform fundamentally different tasks using many different hardware platforms; each distribution can be crafted for a subtly unique crowd. For example, the United States Postal Service uses Linux in large robotic sorting systems connected to Intel-based personal computers to scan and route American mail. On the other hand, a company called Digital Domain used Linux to help render the graphics used in the creation of the movie *Titanic*. At the same time, I use SuSE Linux to write articles, surf the Web and send emails. The Queen also uses Linux to run her Web site **www.royal.gov.uk/index.htm**, shown in Figure 2.2.

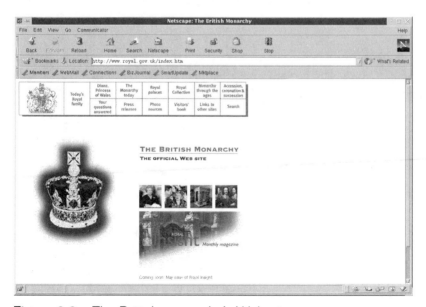

Figure 2.2   The British monarchy's Web site

The existence of so many different Linux distributions gives users the ability to choose the operating system which will best complete the task at hand. Each distribution's heart is still Linux, but the personality will vary according to personal taste or corporate needs.

Are the different distributions compatible?

Generally speaking, yes. Since the kernel (core) of the system and the basic utilities remain similar, binary executables from one Linux distribution can usually be executed without problems on a computer running a separate Linux distribution. That said, there are some notable exceptions to this general rule, most often when discussing the age of the Linux distribution in question or the hardware on which it is operating.

Binary compatibility exceptions

A program 'binary' is the program's executable file. This file is not human-readable, since it's just full of bit after bit of machine code. In Windows, binary files typically end in .exe or .com; in MacOS, binary files are usually referred to as 'applications'.

Linux binaries are generally incompatible with Linux distributions, which were created either much earlier or much later than the program in question. In short, old programs won't work well on new Linux machines, and new programs won't work well on old Linux machines, just as Windows 95 programs won't easily work with Windows 3.1.

Also, binary compatibility does not extend across multiple hardware platforms. Binaries built for Intel-based computers cannot be executed on Macintosh machines. The program in question can still be used; it must simply be recompiled for each platform. Recompiling rarely represents a problem, since nearly all Linux software is free and includes source code, and source code is portable from one Linux machine to the next.

Package compatibility exceptions

'Packages' are normal programs which have been pre-tested to work properly with a specific Linux distribution and then bundled for an automatic install/uninstall utility. This utility is included with the Linux distribution, not with the package itself.

Multiple package formats exist because most distributions choose to create their own. These packages are not compatible across distributions. While this incompatibility may seem like a serious fragmentation of the Linux community, it is not as bad as it at first appears. Most major programs are released in a number of different package formats, one for each of the popular distributions. And nearly all Linux software is also released as a source code 'tarball' which can be compiled and used without the need for an install/uninstall utility.

That said, it should be noted that the users who need Linux to run a specific, single application should buy the distribution to match the application which supports it, and not vice versa.

Source compatibility exceptions

Source code is the set of instructions which, when translated into machine language, make a program which a computer can execute. Source code is written by humans using computer programming languages like C or C++. Linux is different from operating systems like Windows or MacOS in that nearly all source code is available to users at no extra cost, including the code for programs and for the operating system itself.

Linux source code is largely 'portable,' which means that code can be translated into machine language on any Linux computer. There are exceptions to this rule, however; most commonly, these exceptions come with age. As was the case with binary executables above, old Linux source code is less likely to translate correctly into machine language on newer Linux computers, and newer Linux source code is less likely to translate correctly into machine language on older Linux computers.

Tools do exist to make source code more globally portable, and many program authors already make use of these tools to ensure that the code they have created on their machine will easily translate into machine language on your machine. As time progresses, these tools are likely to be used more and more often; we may find that source code compatibility issues become non-existent in the future. Until then, however, if you are planning to compile your own programs (instead of installing programs created by others), the best way to ensure absolute source compatibility from machine to machine is to ensure that both machines run identical Linux distributions.

Which kind of Linux is right for me?

It can be difficult to choose a distribution when so many exist, and aside from the differences between various Linux distributions, users should also remember that Linux is available in multiple forms: as a download, in a book or on a CD-ROM. Which of these distributions and/or formats is right for you? It's your call but I have always come back to SuSE Linux.

How do you want your Linux?

Nearly every Linux distribution is available in several forms. The form in which you acquire your distribution will have a great deal to do with your skill level and stamina as a prospective Linux user.

Linux as an Internet download is potentially strenuous, especially for modem users. Still, for many users, downloading Linux remains the cheapest way to obtain it. Beware that installing a distribution this way requires lots of free hard drive space; the user must have space to store Linux as it is downloaded, and then to install Linux from the downloaded material.

'Glue-in' Linux distributions on CD-ROM are found everywhere – in paperback books, magazines, even as 'bonus disks' which come with other software. Be warned that since these distributions are unofficial copies (though they are completely legal), you may find that they are different from the official distribution by the same name and may, in rare cases, even be incompatible in some way.

Sometimes, such glue-in Linux CD-ROM disks actually contain a 'house brand' distribution of Linux, which does not match the behaviour or package format of any of the major distributions. While these disks do contain fully-fledged Linux operating systems, it is almost certainly better for new users (or newbies) to buy a more common distribution, so that software and technical support will be more forthcoming.

I tend to recommend that users buy a Linux distribution by visiting the official Web page and buying the official disk for whichever distribution they have chosen. Why? Because these distributions are the genuine article; they come with boot floppies and/or install guide texts, and users can be certain that they will receive the full, official, compatible, supported version.

Of course, the official box set of any distribution tends to be more expensive than unofficial versions; in my opinion, the extra security and support are well worth the price for beginners. And the prices may surprise you – even the official versions of Linux distributions are considerably cheaper than their Windows counterparts.

Finally, there are the cheap CDs. These are bare CD-ROM disks, which come in a disk sleeve and nothing else. No boot floppies, no documentation and you're on your own. If you're planning to need any help at all installing Linux, and you can't find a person to give you that help, stick to SuSE Linux.

Is Linux difficult to use?

This is a frequently asked question, perhaps because most people have heard that Linux is similar to UNIX. UNIX has an image problem. Many people think of it as something used by scientists and run on powerful and expensive workstations. However, in several important ways Linux is not like UNIX. Linux runs on personal computers. This means that it is suitable for and aimed at a wider base of users than UNIX. As well as the hardware, the applications software for Linux is developed with a different market in mind. You, the user, are the target for Linux software, not a vague set of development goals.

Another concern with Linux is that it is not like the operating system you are used to. Linux is not MacOS or Windows. But there are similarities as well as differences. All modern operating systems support software to run a windows, icons, mouse, pull-down menus' (WIMP) graphical user interface. Linux is no exception. Using a window manager under Linux is no different to the desktop on other operating systems.

Linux was developed as an operating system from scratch to be lightweight and to run fast. In its early revisions there were no commercial pressures to release improvements. This means that Linux has had a chance to develop a very stable base. It may seem amazing that an operating system written by volunteers would be better than something made by a commercial organisation, but of Linux's results speak for themselves. More hours are probably spent in developing Linux software than any other.

The multi-tasking advantage of Linux

One of the advantages that Linux offers is the speed of the system. Linux is fast and it can do many things at once. The machine does not lock up while files are deleted or a floppy disk is being formatted. Because Linux can do many things at once efficiently, the user can get more done. Getting more done in less time is what usability is all about.

User interfaces

How you interact with the operating system depends on your *user interface*. The keyboard and display screen form an interface between you and the systems hardware. The user interface is between you and the programs you use.

An application's user interface determines its appearance and behaviour. There are two commonly used types of user interfaces for Linux.

- **Graphical user interfaces**
  When a user interface has graphical objects, such as windows and menus, it is called a graphical user interface (GUI). KDE and Gnome provide interfaces between you and your computer.

  The graphical *window system*, which is part of the graphical user interface, organises graphics output on the display and does basic text and graphics drawing functions, very similar to using Microsoft Windows.

- **Command line interface**
  The command line interface (CLI) is also known as the *shell*. This interface is character-based. The screen displays a system prompt, and the commands you type from the keyboard appear next to the prompt.

As well as the GUI discussed above, Linux does have access to a powerful command line interface. This is unsuitable for general use by the majority of users. But for specific tasks or for advanced users like programmers the command line interface or 'shell' is a useful alternative. The shell is only superficially like the old MS-DOS prompt. A shell language has access to dozens of commands and has a richer syntax. Having different ways of doing the same thing provides flexibility as well as adding complexity. You can get things done in the way you want to do them. Again, this is what usability is all about.

Command line interface vs. graphical user interface: pros and cons

The shell (CLI) has a rich set of commands but it is easy to make mistakes. The GUI only has menu commands but it is easy to see what you are doing. The choice is yours. Finally, from a user support point of view, shell commands are often better as they are easier to explain.

Another important usability issue is what to do when you have a problem.

Whether the problem is not knowing the right way to go about a task or a catastrophic hardware failure, the effect is the same. The time taken to resolve problems is time that could be spent in doing productive work. So access to help in all its forms is a key aspect of usability.

Internet support

Linux does not have the expensive and time-consuming telephone support lines that other operating system makers are keen on. Instead from the outset Linux provided and continues to provide all its help as comprehensive documentation with the products (more of this later), and via Internet services. Linux software is supported via a system of email lists and newsgroups. These operate on a 24 hours a day, seven days a week basis. Somewhere in the world there are always some experts around who know how to solve your user problems and can point you in the right direction (see Figures 2.3 and 2.4).

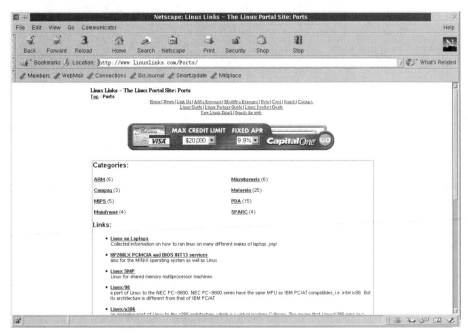

Figure 2.3   Getting information

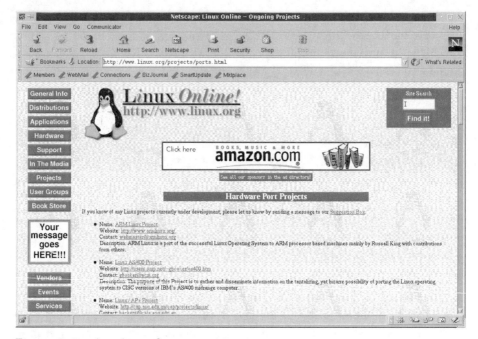

Figure 2.4   Another information site

Just why such experts provide this support is no mystery. First, everyone gets support in the same way so participation seems natural and normal. Second, to become an expert on a particular product does not require going on officially sanctioned courses. To become an expert on a particular software system of Linux you need to read the available documentation, and then apply it in the real world. A good way to gain this experience is the Internet forums, the primary training ground workshops, which is why they are excellent for support.

Documentation

Due to its free availability on the Internet and the liberal distribution of the source code, Linux is probably one of the best documented operating systems available. This is important because documentation is fundamental to understanding any software product. The complex and powerful systems that Linux provides often come with a *lot* of documentation

Virtually any question you can think of has been answered in FAQs, readme files or online text files, as well as in several books. In order to make this information more accessible, SuSE provides the bulk of it in hypertext markup language (HTML) format. When you call up help in a software program, a browser appears on the screen which allows you to read the help file at your own speed. As a special bonus, a support database comes with Linux – also available on the Internet at **http://sdb.suse.de/sdb/ en/html/index.html**, where all common support queries are listed.

Linux software availability

One of the big plus points of Linux is that it has a large body of application programs available, most of them of a high quality and free of charge. But once Linux is installed how do you go about getting them? And how do updates work? Who supports them? Opponents of Linux argue that there are no applications available for the systems to run. The truth is that there is free software available for the Linux OS for almost any task imaginable. While you may not be able to walk into a shop and buy Linux versions of every Windows product, the equivalents are out there, and they are usually less expensive. There are several popular pieces of equivalent software products for the Linux OS, as you will see in this short summary.

Netscape Communicator

Netscape's Web browser has been available for Linux since before version 1.0. It is available from the downloads section of the Netscape Web site. The latest version is Communicator 4.5 and includes Netscape Messenger – a combined mail and news client; Netscape Composer, a graphical HTML authoring tool; and Netscape Navigator the Web browser. Most features found in the Windows version of Communicator work under Linux including Java and Javascript. Several third party plug-ins for features such as video and audio are also available. The Linux version of Communicator is free for both commercial and non-commercial use and is included on the CD of many Linux distributions.

Corel WordPerfect 8.0

The latest version of Corel's flagship word processor, WordPerfect 8, is currently available for Linux. WordPerfect has been available for Linux from third parties since version 6, but with version 8 Corel has decided to make it available for download on the Web. Information about Corel's commitment to Linux and instructions on downloading WordPerfect can be found at **http://linux.corel.com**. Most features of the Windows version of WordPerfect are available in the Linux version, including the spelling and grammar check, the Internet publisher and the ability to read MS Word 97 files. Some features are not available in the version on the Web, including the font installer, equation editor and drawing tools. A commercial version is available containing these missing features.

The GIMP

The GIMP is a piece of image editing software similar to Adobe's Photoshop. It was originally developed for the UNIX/Linux platform by a group of programmers on the Internet. It is available for free download, including source code, from **www.gimp.org**. Over 20 different types of file formats are supported by GIMP including JPEG and TIFF. Many types of image operations are supported including layers, colour balance and normalising. GIMP also includes its own scripting language, allowing advanced users to programme their own macros and filters.

3

Linux Applications and the Desktop

T his chapter discusses the specialised software applications that can be run on Linux, their features and capabilities, and two of the Linux desktop environments, K Desktop Environment and GNOME, touching on the similarities they share with other operating systems as well as the differences.

The Linux desktop environment: KDE and GNOME

Did you know that...?

Window

A window is a rectangular screen segment, usually decorated by a frame. This frame normally contains decorations, which can change the window's size, move the window and alter other window properties. In order to work with windows, an X Server and a Window manager must be running.

The K Desktop Environment (KDE) (Figure 3.1) and GNOME (Figure 3.2) provide a complete graphical environment under X. On top of a window manager, they also contain applications such as file manager, editors, viewers and even some games. All these applications have a consistant look and feel, that is, all window elements such as button and menu bars look the same.

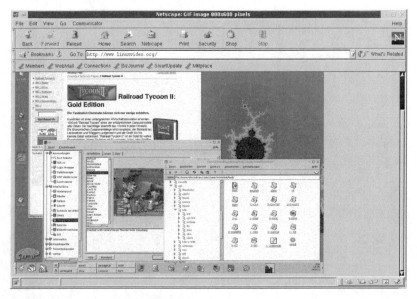

Figure 3.1 A KDE desktop

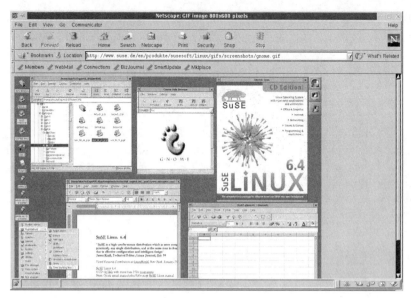

Figure 3.2 A GNOME desktop

KDE and GNOME eliminate the cumbersome editing of configuration files. Colours, fonts, menu bars and buttons can be changed using graphical configuration tools, and both desktops support 'drag and drop'.

X Window

In addition to the command line, the so called shell, Linux also provides a graphical user interface (GUI). The X Window System (often simply referred to as X or X11), the standard for graphical user interfaces under UNIX, has been developed continuously and has been ported by the XFree86 project team onto PC UNIX systems.

Unlike so many other GUIs, X11 is based on the client/server model. The X server runs locally on a system, handles all access to the graphics hardware and processes user input via mouse and keyboard. The applications are the so-called X Clients which communicate directly with the server.

Did you know that...?

Command line

Working with UNIX in a shell is a command line-oriented process. This means that any process you enter in a shell can have its own command line (for example, the command ls can take a lot of options to change its behaviour).

It doesn't matter whether the X Clients are executed locally, that is, on the machine at which you are working, or remotely on another system in the network. In the latter case, only the screen output of the program is transferred via the network to the local machine; all processing is carried out on the remote system. This makes it possible for all application programs in a network to be run on a powerful application server while the client systems can just be simple terminals. This configuration saves not only the high costs of new hardware, but also reduces administration and maintenance costs for the network.

Another special feature of the X Window system is its window management. On a graphical user interface, all applications are displayed in windows. With X Window, the look (frames, size, colours, buttons, and so on) and feel (placement of icons and texture) are not controlled by the X Server, but by a window manager.

Figure 3.3   One of SuSE Linux's window managers

What might at first sound confusing soon appears to be a major advantage when you take a closer look: the SuSE Linux package provides more than ten different window managers, allowing the user to create the look and feel of his interface himself. It goes without saying that under Linux every window manager is in itself freely configurable (Figure 3.3).

In larger varied networks, the availability of several window managers makes it possible to create a single interface across several hardware architectures. fvwm95 and qvwm are two window managers available which have been designed along the lines of the Windows 95 interface.

To facilitate the configuration of the individual window managers for users, SuSE has developed a tool called *susewm*, which does away with the cumbersome editing of configuration files to a large extent. Depending on the programs installed, susewm automatically generates pop-up menus. From these menus, one can then conveniently start X applications. As susewm covers more than seven window managers, you can change window managers at any time using the appropriate menus. SuSE Linux provides a completely preconfigured fvwm2, the most commonly used window manager under Linux, enabling you to start work immediately.

Internet

The Internet is a worldwide network of interconnected computers. Machines are accessed via their IP addresses, which are unique. These IP addresses are structured in a hierarchical manner. There are top-level and national domains, domains, sub-domains and the addresses of each individual machine. Together with the numerical IP address (such as 192.168.0.1), there are aliases (such as helios.cosmos.com), which simplify the IP address for the user. It is not only the hardware layer that keeps the Internet up and running, but also a system of protocols (such as FTP, HTTP, TCP) operating on specific logical layers. Well-known services of the Internet are email and the World Wide Web (WWW or W3). A very important keyword in connection with Internet communication is netiquette, which encourages people to behave politely and makes sure that everything runs smoothly.

Protocol

Protocols organise communication between the different machines in networks, either on hardware or software. They specify the format of the data to be transferred, which machines have control over others, and so on. Such protocols include FTP, UDP, TCP and HTTP.

Whether you are talking about your company-wide intranet or the world-wide Internet, Linux is the right choice of platform for your WWW server. The SuSE distribution contains the WWW server apache: **www.apache.org/** (Figure 3.4).

Nearly one in two servers on the Internet use this versatile and powerful WWW server. It boasts extensive functionality and is highly configurable, allowing you to accomplish all your requirements. With the help of *squid*, the proxy server, frequently requested documents can be held locally. This reduces Internet traffic and speeds up access to frequently used documents.

Linux is also highly suitable as a mail and news server, being able to act as such in assorted networks. You can even continue to use Microsoft Exchange on a Windows client.

There will soon be a shortage of Internet protocol (IP) addresses on the Internet. Although Internet service providers (ISPs) can only supply a small number of addresses, SuSE Linux supports IP-masquerading in order to link up a whole network to the Internet. This means that a single machine router will take care of the correct routing of all network traffic.

Security

By using a firewall, SuSE Linux protects your network from unwanted visitors. The packet filter integrated into the kernel allows for flexible adaptation to local requirements. Incoming as well as outgoing IP traffic can be restricted.

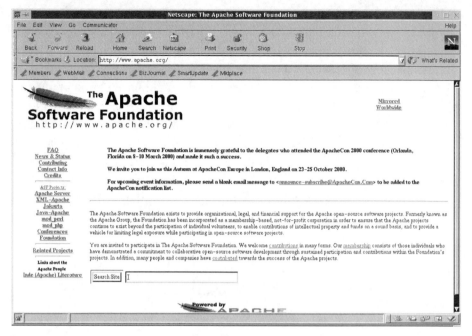

Figure 3.4 The Apache Software Foundation

Programming development environment

Because of the association between source codes and the availability of the standard user interface OSF-Motif, Linux represents an ideal development platform for applications in the UNIX area. Platform-independent graphical 2D and 3D applications can be developed using MetroLink's OpenGL.

SuSE Linux provides compilers for all common programming languages. With GNU C/C++ you have one of the best compilers on the market at your disposal. The graphical debugging tool *xxgdb* lets you identify errors easily under X11.

Did you know that...?

Environment

A shell normally provides some kind of environment where you can temporarily set options such as paths of programs, the user name, the current path, the appearance of the prompt and so on. This data is stored in an environment variable. These variables can be assigned, for example, by the shell's configuration files.

In order to keep programming as simple and convenient as possible, SuSE Linux contains the sophisticated editor *GNU emacs* (as well as its X Window counterpart, *xemacs*). Emacs offers a special mode for virtually every programming language, where the editor itself formats the programming code. Thanks to the highlighting of certain key words in colour the programmer has a good overview at all times. But emacs is more than a simple editor. Virtually all the tasks that can be carried out under Linux can also be handled using emacs, including the reading of email and news, surfing the Net, using file transfer protocol (FTP) to transfer files or even creating simple drawings. Emacs is easily programmable and executing keyboard macros is also possible.

Should you still prefer another editor, you have plenty of choice. SuSE Linux offers more than ten editors, including *vi*, the classic UNIX editor.

Text processing

With TeX or LaTeX2e, SuSE Linux offers a sophisticated text processing system, which is well established in the scientific and the publishing world. If you have ever tried to create a document consisting of several hundred pages with a standard word processing system, you know why you need LaTeX2e.

TeX is an interpreter that works similarly to a setter at a printing company. Even the very complex setting of mathematical formulae is no problem for TeX. Contrary to the usual WYSIWYG (what you see is what you get) word processing you enter your text in TeX as ASCII text with the appropriate formatting commands in a standard editor. The resulting file is then compiled by the TeX interpreter.

With the LaTeX package, SuSE Linux provides an extensive collection of TeX programs and utilities. Furthermore, you will find tools for the creation of LaTeX graphics (*xfig, texcad*), shells (*ts, xtem*) and converters (*detex, LaTeX2HTML, tex2html*). To make the switch to TeX even easier, SuSE Linux also contains the program *LyX*, a WYSIWYG word processor based on TeX/LaTeX. Check it out at **www.lyx.org/** (see Figure 3.5).

There are also professional office solutions under Linux, with which all tasks can be carried out. SuSE offers the well-established package Applixware 4.4.2 as part of the Linux Office Suite. SuSE Linux also contains StarOffice 5.1 Personal Edition and WordPerfect 8 Download Edition – the use of these products for personal purposes is free.

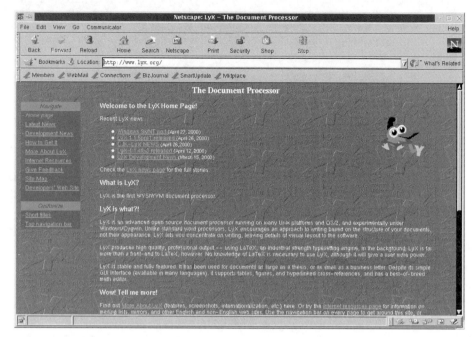

Figure 3.5 The LyX home page

Graphics

A whole range of image processing and graphics programs is available for Linux. The best known is *The Gimp* (see Figure 3.6), at **www.gimp.org/**.

Gimp is an image processing program very similar to commercial programs. The shareware program *xv*, one of the most popular Linux programs, offers a similarly broad functionality. Pictures in more than 20 different graphic formats can be displayed and processed.

Simple pictures can be created very quickly with *Xpaint*. *Xfig* is a very powerful program for the creation of vector graphics, which can be linked directly into TeX documents. Professional 3D graphics are best created with raytracers, such as Povray (**www.povray.org**), shown in Figure 3.7. Raytracing applications take a 'model' with a description of a scene, or a text editor, and generate image files from the model. Raytracers usually take into consideration lighting, cameras position/angle, material textures and other properties affecting the images.

Even the viewing of films is no problem with Linux. *Xanim* and *mpegplay* run films in all common formats (mpeg, avi, Quicktime and so on).

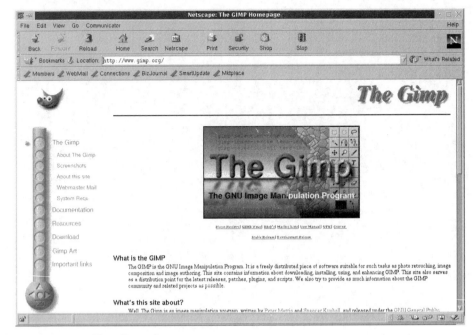

Figure 3.6   The Gimp home page

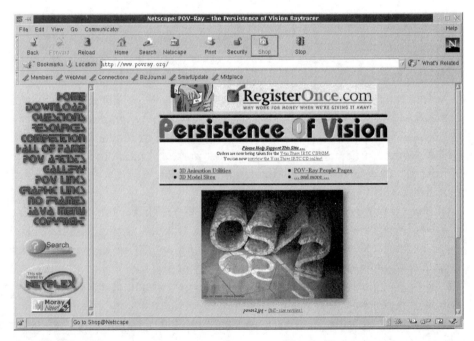

Figure 3.7   Povray

Sound

MIDI-Sequencer, WAV-Player and Audiotracer turn your SuSE Linux machine into a sound studio. You can also listen to music CDs while you are working. The Motif CD-Player *xmcd* comes with a database which automatically recognises artist, titles and tracks of several thousand CDs. Using *speakf*, you can even talk over a TCP/IP network (Internet).

Emulators

An emulator is a program that mimics the software and hardware of another computer or game system. Emulators are programs that allow you to emulate other terminals in order to run specific software on the Linux operating system.

Instead of rewriting Windows applications for Linux, which requires massive coding, various workarounds are available, including WINE (discussed briefly below and in more detail in Chapter 5.)

WINE (**www.winehq.com**), software that lets Windows programs run on Linux machines, provides both a development toolkit for porting Windows source code to Linux and a program loader, which allows unmodified Windows 3.1/95/NT binaries (compiled programs) to run under popular Intel UNIX operating systems, including Linux, FreeBSD and Solaris.

Corel, also using WINE with help from Cygnus, demonstrated a Quattro Pro spreadsheet running flawlessly under WINE at the recent LinuxWorld Conference and Expo.

'WINE is still under development and is not suitable for general use,' warns WINE project leader Alexandre Julliard (**www.winehq.com/Apps/query.cgi**). But more than 1200 applications have been tested with WINE, with varying results.

There are a great many emulators in Linux: SuSE Linux offers no fewer than 14. The most interesting is surely the DOS emulator, *dosemu*. Strictly speaking, this is not a DOS emulator, but a BIOS emulator which allows you to start DOS under Linux. You can even run some DOS programs which use protected mode.

Also, you will find m68K-emulators for ATARI ST (*StonX*) and Amiga A500 in SuSE Linux. Using the Z80 emulator you can emulate a Gameboy under Linux and run all the Gameboy games! Sinclair ZX81 and ZX Spectrum machines, as well as the game consoles Coleco Vision and ColecoADAM, can also be emulated under Linux using Z80. See the section on emulators in Chapter 5 for more details.

Was your first computer a Commodore? Thanks to the emulator *Vice* which emulates Commodore 64, Commodore 128, VC20 and Commodore Pet, you can get out all those old programs again.

If you enjoy playing games then you should look at the emulators for game consoles. In 1977 Atari launched the video console system VCS 2600. Today it can be emulated using Stella. NES (Nintendo Entertainment System) owners will also find their own emulation.

Note that for most of the emulators you will need additional CD-ROMs, which for copyright reasons UNIX is not allowed to include on their CD. In order to boot the DOS emulation under Linux, you require a DOS licence, i.e. MS-DOS, Windows 95 (MS-DOS 7), IBM PC-DOS, DR-DOS, Caldera OpenDOS or FreeDOS. Licences are available from Microsoft for £160.

4

The Practicalities of Linux

Where to find free software ■

How do I install free software? ■

Migrating from Microsoft to Linux ■

Linux hardware ■

Linux device drivers ■

T his chapter discusses the ways in which you can obtain Linux software, including pointers to useful and informative Web sites. It then goes on to describe how to install it, avoiding any installation problems, the best way to migrate from one operating system (Microsoft) to another (Linux), and ends with a section on Linux hardware, device drivers and applications.

Where to find free software

FTP and Web sites

There are many Internet sites that carry Linux software. They do not charge for downloads or require you as a user to make uploads in exchange. Three types of organisation run these sites: first, the volunteers who write the programs for their own use. Their primary aim is to promote use of their programs and to get feedback from other users to help them improve the programs. Second, companies like SuSE who distribute full working sets of Linux software. Although companies like this derive little direct income from their Web sites, the Internet provides a fast and cheap way to deliver updates to their customers. It also attracts new ones by offering complete software programs free of charge. Third, there are other organisations such as universities who have an interest in the free flow of software. The differences between the sites in terms of the core software they carry are not great and can again be split into three categories. Some very large sites carry many unusual programs. There are well-organised sites that make it easy to find the materials. Finally, there are specialist sites that focus on a particular area of interest or concentrate on leading-edge Linux software technology.

CD-ROM distributions

There are also CD-ROMs available containing large sets of programs. The better ones are produced by groups interested in a particular program or by distribution makers. An example is the POVray CD for 3D graphics. There are also several sets of CDs available, which aim to be comprehensive, and hold a tremendous amount of software on 10 volumes or more. However, unless you have some expertise, they can be a waste of time, as they are sometimes badly organised.

How do I install free software?

Package managers

In the early days of Linux simply producing a working system took a great deal of work in obtaining the correct programs. Usually the user would have to spend time compiling the programs. Much technical know-how was required to get the simplest things to work. Modern Linux systems have overcome these problems. The main tool they use is a system called a *package manager*. Package managers know how different programs interact. Take the example of installing a working email server. The package manager will check for Internet connectivity before installing the mail program. If the necessary software is not installed it will automatically install it or stop with an error. Package managers know how to install most available programs. The people writing the package add this information. They examine the program and bundle extra information and even set up scripts with it. The package manager then uses this extra information to install software automatically.

This extra information will include data on the version numbers and facilities the program offers so keeping up to date is easy with a package manager. Finding and installing Linux software is easy with the aid of the package management software. All the major distributions offer something. The crudest and oldest is the Slackware installpkg program. Red Hat's RPM system is more sophisticated and is the most widely used. Debian distributions include several tools including apt, dpkg and dselect that together act as a powerful package system.

The one major problem that Linux does currently face is with commercially available software. Although Linux is strong in free software, if you have a favourite commercial package you would like to use under Linux you may have to wait for it. Currently many manufacturers are promising Linux versions but there are not as many applications available for Linux as there are for Microsoft Windows.

In terms of usability, this is a real problem, as switching to an alternative program can affect productivity. The solution is in the hands of the applications software makers. Given the many advantages of Linux, software makers are turning to it. It is only a matter of time before Linux becomes a major market for commercial software and free software.

Migrating From Microsoft to Linux

Moving from Windows 98 to Linux? How would you go about starting a project such as this? That depends on which applications you need. If you are just doing Web services and Internet stuff, you can remove Windows from your computer; the Linux tools are much better. If you depend on Word, Excel or PowerPoint, then you should install Linux on a spare partition and investigate the local equivalents. StarOffice and Applix supply Linux office suites that can read and write Word and Excel documents as well as carry out PowerPoint-like tasks. There are also individual programs, such as AbiWord (which will read and write Word files), Gnumeric (for Excel), and MagicPoint (for PowerPoint).

I think that Linux makes a great platform for either the desktop or the server environment, but I do have to mention that compatibility with Microsoft products is often a problem. This issue is not unique to Linux, by any means, but has been common to vendors such as Corel, Lotus and others through the years. The problem is that Microsoft does not remain compatible with *themselves* on internal file formats. I am not sure if this is because they have such an unclear strategy that they cannot come up with an extendible storage format for each of their office products, or if it is a deliberate attempt to frustrate the competition from re-engineering their products, but it is a continual problem. I recently encountered this problem, not on Linux, but using Windows 98. I installed Office 97, Corel's WordPerfect 2000 suite, and StarOffice 5.1. I was able to do many simple functions across all three suites, but when I started to embed drawings and charts from various office components into a Word document, I ran into problems with reading and correctly interpreting the embedded contents within my documents.

It is not a Linux compatibility problem, as such, that I see, but a problem in exchanging file formats between the numerous office products. If you stick to simple documents, a fair degree of compatibility can be found. Both Applix and StarOffice have good Linux application suites, and work as well as any others. Corel is also doing good work in this area. Perhaps the open source community should build a *new* set of compatible office products and end this problem of standardisation of files. You will find ways to overcome this in the VMware section in Chapter 5.

Things you should know before you install Linux

Linux was originally developed for the PC but it is now available on almost every hardware platform. You can order Linux for Alpha-stations, Sparc, m68k machines (Amiga, Atari, Motorola), PowerPCs, Apple PowerMac and ARM-based systems (for example, Acorn RiscPC). See **www.linuxlinks.com/Ports/** for more information.

The ease of installation of SuSE Linux has evolved at a tremendous rate in the last six months and I believe you will find it very easy to install using YaST2, which is available since version SuSE Linux 6.3. The following are a few points you should note.

Get your hardware information

Before you commit to SuSE Linux, check out the SuSE Web site **http://cdb.suse.de/cdb_english.html** (Figure 4.1) for a hardware compatibility list. Make sure all of the peripherals and components you need to use are listed. If you already run Windows on the PC you would like to install Linux on, go into the Device Manager (right-click `My Computer`, click the `Device Manager` tab, and select `Print`). Choose to print out 'All devices and system summary.' This data can be useful if you are asked for specific information about your hardware.

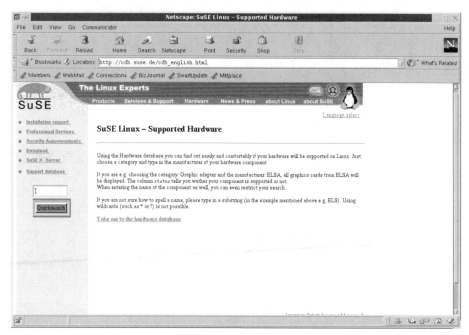

Figure 4.1 Hardware information

Memory

The memory is the brain of your machine. In Linux, one often refers to two different types of memory: physical memory and virtual memory. Physical memory is made up of a number of memory (RAM) chips. RAM varies from 8Mb up to 128Mb on a typical PC. High-performance computers may have 1Gb or more of RAM.

Virtual (or logical) memory is a concept that, when implemented by a computer and its operating system, allows programmers to use a very large range of memory or storage addresses for stored data. The computing system maps the programmer's virtual addresses to real hardware storage addresses. Usually, the programmer is freed from having to be concerned about the availability of data storage.

In addition to managing the mapping of virtual stroage addresses to real storage addresses, a computer implementing virtual memory or storage also manages storage swapping between active storage (RAM) and hard disk or other high-volume storage devices. Data is read in units called 'pages' of sizes ranging from a thousand bytes up to several megabytes in size. This reduces the amount of physical storage access that is required and speeds up overall system performance.

Backup

Backups should be done regularly, especially for important files! It is also worthwhile backing up your configuration files. In Linux, one of the commands used for backups is `tar`. It backs up the files to a device or filename. Quite often `tar` is used in combination with gzip.

Test the water

If you have an extra PC with no critical programs or data on it, you might want to use it as your Linux guinea pig. If you have an old 486, Linux will give it a new lease of life and allow you to experiment without running the risk of damaging any files on your main computer.

Know your resource needs

Make sure you have enough hard disk space, RAM and CPU speed to accommodate and handle a Linux install – either on its own or in separate hard disk partitions on your Windows PC. Check the Hardware site in Figure 4.1, ascertain your hardware resource requirements and then see what your PC has available.

Have a spare floppy disk ready

Most distributions will prompt you to create a rescue disk installation. Have a blank floppy disk ready to carry out this important step.

Back up your data

To be on the safe side, back up all your important data on removable media before beginning the Linux installation.

Linux hardware

One question that often comes up is what do I need to look for when buying a PC to run Linux on? A quick answer is, if you already run Windows on a PC, you have everything you need to run Linux. It is not always accurate, but it describes the CPU, disk and memory requirements fairly well: Linux needs no more of any of these than Windows, and can often get away with less. A sensible minimum specification these days is a P200, with 64Mb of RAM, and at least 1Gb of disk space – today you'll be hard-pressed to buy a new machine with less.

But that is not where the story ends. Not all PC hardware is Linux-friendly. The first and biggest problem is equipment that relies on Windows software to make up for some sort of deficiency. Winmodems are a case in point. Most modems have a built-in microprocessor and ROM of their own; you can plug them into just about any computer and they will work. Not so with Winmodems; much of their processing work is farmed out to a set of Windows drivers that run on the PC. No Windows? No modem, then.

Similar warnings apply to some printers; indeed, it is prudent to be suspicious of any hardware gadget with 'Win' as a prefix to its name. It is not necessarily incompatible, but it is a sign that you should double-check before spending money on it.

Probably the most important item is your hard disk subsystem: the drives and controllers. At this point it is worth mentioning a simple law – SCSI rules. SCSI (Small Computer Systems Interface) is a standard bus that Macintoshes and other platforms have used for many years in preference to such PC-specific items as IDE, EIDE, or the venerable ST-506 interface. Most PC motherboards don't have built-in SCSI controllers; you usually buy them as separate boards. Furthermore, SCSI drives tend to cost more than EIDE drives; in general, prices are about a year behind in terms of the price/capacity ratio. However, SCSI kit is generally of higher performance. In particular, the SCSI bus permits asynchronous commands; your computer can send a stream of read/write requests to the drive without waiting for each one to complete in turn. While modern UDMA drives probably outclass older SCSI kit (certainly pre-SCSI-3), a machine equipped with an SCSI drive easily outperforms equivalent EIDE-dependent kit. Linux does not treat its storage in the way Windows does; it is very file system intensive, and it is under these conditions that SCSI hardware outshines the opposition.

Another advantage of SCSI is that it is possible to daisy-chain devices in an SCSI chain. On my PC there are two hard disks, a CD writer, a CD-ROM jukebox, a DAT drive and a scanner; and it all works off a single controller card.

Next most important is the display system. As a general rule of thumb, expect to run the X11 windowing system and some sort of desktop like KDE. Realistically, you will want a fairly fast video card with at least 4Mb of video RAM – however, you will need to ensure this is supported. SuSE Linux are supporting leading-edge graphics boards; the XSuSE servers can be found at **www.suse.de/en/support/xsuse/index.html** (*see* Figure 4.2).

It goes without saying that a good monitor is its own reward. After all, you have only one pair of eyes!

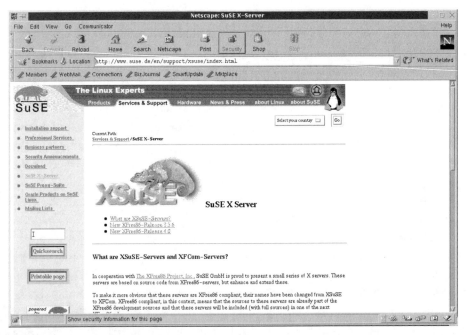

Figure 4.2   XSuSE servers information

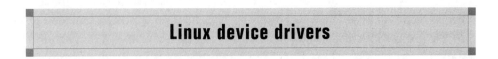

Linux device drivers

To begin to understand how device drivers operate and how to use them, you must first forget everything you know about installing device drivers in Windows. While deep below the surface Linux handles devices in a similar manner as Windows, you will find that the process of installing and accessing hardware in Linux is quite different.

That said, this is a simplified explanation of how device drivers are used in Linux. In Linux, device drivers are implemented in one of three ways.

The kernel

In this case, support for the device already exists in the kernel itself. Under normal circumstances the device will be automatically detected, assigned a basic configuration and made available to the rest of the system. Typically the kernel will provide direct support for the hardware necessary to mount the root file system. The following hardware is supported in this way: standard VGA monitor, generic IDE controllers and disks, motherboard devices and chipsets, serial ports and parallel ports.

Kernel modules

A kernel module is a portion of the kernel that exists as a separate file. When loaded into the running kernel, the module provides the kernel additional functionality. In an effort to reduce the resources consumed by the kernel, non-critical devices are supported by kernel 'modules'. Modules can be dynamically loaded and unloaded as necessary.

Modules also provide more flexibility, since they can be independently configured and reconfigured without rebooting the system. This flexibility allows us to use more user-friendly applications to configure the modules, as the system is already running in basic form.

Modules are often used for devices such as soundcards, SCSI adapters and network interface cards (NICs).

Did you know that...?

Mass storage media

A collection of different media for storing data. Typical mass storage media are floppy disks, hard drives, streamer tapes, CD-ROMs, magneto-optical disks, holographic media and many more.

Applications

In some cases, both the kernel and an application handle devices. The kernel is responsible for the parallel port for printers, while the application provides its own driver to handle the specifics of that printer.

Other examples of this include modems, CD-ROMs and X Windows.

For more information visit **http://cdb.suse.de/cgi-bin/scdb?HTML= ENGLISH/cdb_listtemplates/menu.htm&LANG=ENGLISH** (Figure 4.3).

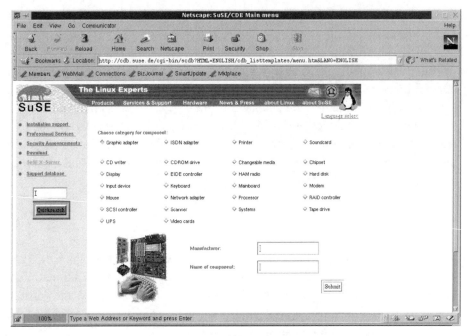

Figure 4.3 Kernel and application information

5

Linux Fact and Fiction

The LINUX FUD factor: fear, uncertainty and doubt

Linux is growing in popularity and, as a consequence, is finding its way into everyday conversation and media articles. Unfortunately, much of this information is either misconstrued or ill informed. This chapter presents some of the more frequently cited myths about Linux and open source software in general and some insights into what is really happening in the Linux world.

'Free/open source software is unreliable'

This phrase always makes people think of software that is given away at no cost, has no owner, and thus has no support or warranty. In reality the 'free' in free software means that the source code has been liberated and anybody may copy and compile it, but that does not exclude payment. As the Free Software Foundation, FSF, originators of the GNU licence put it: 'Think free speech not free beer.'

Most people using Linux for real applications are using commercial distributions, which they have paid for. They thus expect, and get, the same level of quality and support as with any other commercial product. As so much confusion has been caused by use of the term free, many developers now prefer to use the term 'open source'.

'Linux is a UNIX clone cut down to run on a PC'

Linux is not cut down. It is fully fledged and continues to evolve with the latest developments in the software industry.

'Why compromise just to save a few pounds?'

Many Linux users use words like flexible, open, reliable and efficient to describe Linux. Few people use it to save money, although most acknowledge that a lot of money can be saved. At the outset many Linux users were people who wanted to play with UNIX at home but could not afford the workstation costs. But Linux soon grew beyond that.

But money issues are mostly about commercial use. If corporate staff are familiar with one OS and not Linux, setting up a server with Linux will probably cost more, as savings on the operating system price are absorbed by time spent on the learning curve. But once installed and set up, Linux systems require low maintenance, and subsequent systems will require less time and consequently save money. But beyond saving a few pounds, the licence issue goes further. Many system administrators prefer the thin server approach, where services are spread across multiple low-cost machines rather than centred on big central boxes, with the load being split by service rather than users. This approach is more easily scalable and limits downtime. It also makes it easier to upgrade and maintain individual system elements. But if you need per user licences on each box, it can become an economic non-starter. Linux not only makes the thin server model financially viable, but its high efficiency means that older desktop machines no longer considered good enough may be recycled as non-critical servers and routers.

'Linux is neither warrantied nor supported'

Which software products do have warranties? Most software is sold on an 'as is' agreement, and it is up to the user to check that the software is suitable for the application. Commercial distributions of Linux are widely available, and include support options. They offer the same kind of contract as other commercial packages and there is no reason to differentiate these products just because they have an open source base.

On the other hand, users of open source software do have the source, so they may put in that little bug fix or enhancement they need. If they think their enhancement may be useful to others, they release it to be folded back into the main Linux release.

No software is all things to all men, and many people who swear by Linux do so because in the past they have found themselves locked into a system that is not doing all they want, but the necessary 'fix' has not been forthcoming or, as is more often the case, it finally arrives bundled into a paid-for upgrade which includes many other new but undesired elements with a new set of bugs. Linux allows users to configure the system to do what they want it to do.

'Software developers are reluctant to develop for a platform that requires them to release the source code'

That would be understandable, but there is *no* obligation for software developers to release the source of their software, nor is there any obligation to allow the software to be freely copied. There is no difference between selling software for Linux and for any other platform. Open source software developers recognise the need for commercial elements in the system; they believe it is the core code, the application interfaces and the system utilities that must be open in order to get a truly non-proprietary system, extendible by all.

At the same time, all would agree that commercial distributors are necessary in order to package the software into an end-user package with logos, manuals, phone support and so on. As such, the open source software community welcomes and encourages companies to work alongside them selling services, packages and support, as well as interfacing and integrating 'licenced' software with freely available packages. There are many companies that have risen to the challenge of this new market, and they are making healthy profits.

'Linux is fragmenting'

There is no credible evidence that this is happening. Although the commercial Linux distributors differentiate their products, they are compatible and the various companies work together in a friendly manner that is uncommon in the software world. They adhere to a common *filesystem hierarchy standard*, which determines the layout of the system, and they use kernels and libraries from the same series. The misconception that a stand-alone package has to be distributed in a different version for each Linux distribution is brought about by FUD.

Did you know that...?

File system

A file system is a system for structuring files. There are many file systems available which differ (sometimes considerably) in performance and power. Some file systems are strictly tied to certain media.

'Linux has no direction'

Linus Torvalds, the honorary president of the Linux movement, has clearly stated that the long-term goal of Linux is world domination. So Linux is no different to other major operating systems except in that his goal is not for financial remuneration but for the good of society.

'Linux is made up of a lot of little groups running in different directions'

Linux is made up of lots of little groups running in the same direction. A number of mechanisms ensure this. The most important is perhaps the Internet; people working on Linux projects are constantly in discussion with each other by means of newsletters and Web sites, so everybody knows what everybody else is up to. Somebody starting a new project can look at the main Linux Web sites to see if anybody is already doing something related, and they can post their ideas to newsletters to get feedback and input from developers of the mechanisms to which the project will interface. This informal approach, for the most part, works satisfactorily. Two formal mechanisms also exist to resolve conflict. All patches to the Linux kernel pass through the president of the Linux kernel, Linus Torvalds, and so he has the final say on what does and does not go in. He also holds the trademark on the Linux name. I use the term 'president' because Linus does not wholly own Linux. The copyright of each piece of software remains with the authors, but they have to release the software with a licence that permits free copying and updating for it to become a standard part of the kernel, though not for a Linux application used only by themselves.

Nobody can 'own' Linux and, in the event of Linus being unavailable, there are a large number of other developers sufficiently engaged in kernel development to be able to fulfil the presidential post. Another mechanism is Linux International, a non-profit umbrella group for Linux-related organisations that is supported by its commercial members. Members of Linux International include commercial Linux distributors such as Red Hat and SuSE, applications software companies such as Sun and Netscape, and hardware companies from a systems level, such as Compaq, and peripheral manufacturers such as Adaptec. Like other industrial umbrella groups, Linux International derives its authority from the fact that member organisations bind to its conclusions on Linux-related matters. A board voted for by the members controls it.

'Linux is not a technology leader; it is just playing "catch-up"'

This is a bit like saying NASA is just another aerospace company. Certainly the Linux community does not make splash announcements about what it *will* be doing, nor does it make roadmaps so far into the future that when the dates finally arrive everybody has forgotten what they were promised. Linux is all about people doing what they want to do. The openness of Linux makes it very suitable as a 'lab bench' for testing out new ideas, and the reputation of the Linux kernel programmers makes introducing new techniques a personal challenge. Linux was running in 64-bit on the DEC Alpha from day one. It also runs in 64-bit on Sun platforms. It supports SMP, and can be clustered. You can connect a room full of cheap dual-Pentium processors together to make a low-cost supercomputer. The rendering of the film *Titanic* was done by 100 Alpha computers running 64-bit Linux round the clock for several months. When people started using Linux on portables, PCMCIA and power-saving soon found its way into stable kernels. Generally speaking, new technologies and techniques find their way into the development kernels very quickly, often before they are available for other OSs. New technologies that are much sought after by end users are likely to be made available as 'unofficial kernel patches', so that end users may try out new (beta) toys with otherwise stable kernels. If demand is high, the new toy will get a lot of use and hence be quickly debugged sufficiently to be a standard element in the stable kernel releases. If, as sometimes happens, the new idea is unwanted, it just disappears and may never appear as a feature in a stable release.

'The kernel may be advanced, but the applications are old "second-hand" ports'

Linux users make a good deal of use of tried and trusted UNIX applications that have been ported to Linux; they are well known and extremely reliable. But Linux's excellence as a software development platform has made it first choice amongst programmers, and a look through Linux archives will show a multitude of innovative ideas. Most of these are not yet developed enough for practical use, and of course most 'innovation' does not bear fruit. Next-generation software is far more likely to come from a Linux platform than any other OS.

'Linux is insecure'

Linux is, strictly speaking, a kernel, and an OS kernel is intrinsically secure, since it has no means on its own of communicating with the outside world. Break-ins occur via support programs that offer specific network services, and it is in these programs that weaknesses normally occur. Linux security may be considered no different to UNIX security in general.

   The Linux community takes security seriously. Many Linux systems are in the front line and would not last long if problems were not properly addressed. When security alerts are issued, fixes arrive very quickly. Linux distributors, consultants and large sites where Linux is deployed have people dedicated to security and, as ever in the Linux world, these people collaborate. At the same time the basic motto of Linux is flexibility and user choice. You can make or buy a secure system with Linux.

The Microsoft perspective

Microsoft has thrown out a challenge to the biggest threat to its Windows NT operating system, listing reasons why it considers NT to be a better operating system than rival Linux. The single page titled *Linux Myths* is published by Microsoft on its Windows NT server Web site. You can find it at **www.microsoft.com/ntserver/nts/news/msnw/LinuxMyths.asp**. This page sums up its assessment of Linux by saying the operating system 'is not suitable for mainstream usage by business or home users'.

Linux counter-FUD site is launched

A Linux counter-FUD site (Figure 5.1) is available at **http://noFUD. linuxtoday.com**.

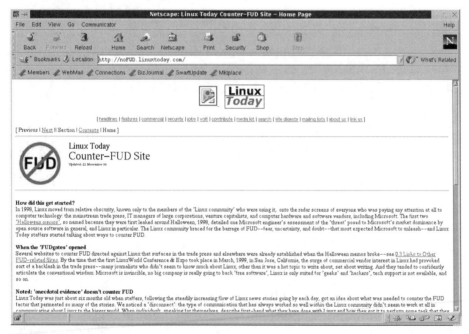

Figure 5.1   Linux's counter-FUD site

The reality behind the myths

As I sifted through the news stories, sorting and summarising the material that related to FUD, I was continually amazed by the effect of the results.

The scale of the change that has to happen for Linux to take the place of Windows

People in the Linux community have been talking about 'world domination' for some time now. Just how seriously people take this, and in what timeframe, is hard to judge. But the magnitude of the change that would have to happen in order for Linux to replace Windows is one of those things that has a writer searching for words that would do them justice. Laying out the scale of Microsoft's market dominance is the only way to describe it.

90% of computers in the world

Windows runs about 90 per cent of all the computers in the world. The standard productivity applications for businesses worldwide are Microsoft Word, Excel and PowerPoint, and most large corporations have major investments in customisations that would be expensive to port if they considered switching.

Microsoft Outlook powers the email servers and clients for most of the businesses using Microsoft Windows and Office. Windows NT now handles file and print sharing in most of these same businesses. And for most, Microsoft Back Office takes care of much of what remains.

Developer Tools Microsoft 'Visual' developer tools are used in a large proportion of application development, in applications both for resale and for internal use. And the 'tight integration' between all the Microsoft products makes it easy for corporate IT departments to stitch together any and all of the pieces to create large, complex systems with relatively little effort.

Applications The vast majority of application programs are available on Windows. Most application programs are released first on Windows, and then ported to other platforms, if they are ported at all. Many Internet browser plug-ins are available only in Windows-specific versions.

UNIX under siege The only areas still holding out against the Microsoft juggernaut are very high-end servers and engineering workstations that run UNIX, and Microsoft has been promising that NT 5, now renamed Windows 2000, will take away a big chunk of that market.

So even if alternative technology somehow emerges, and is clearly superior to a Microsoft product on all counts, the sheer scale, scope, magnitude, whatever you choose to call it, of the change that would have to take place for any alternative to a Microsoft product to present a serious challenge to this market dominance is absolutely mind boggling. Even more so for Linux, when you consider that switching from proprietary software to open source is a much bigger change than just switching vendors: open source requires any commercial vendor who wants to make money from it to make big changes to their business model, and it requires any corporate IT department that adopts it to make big changes to the way they deploy and support software.

Change is underway

However, this change to Linux is happening. A change of incredible proportions has been underway since early 1999, when the number of commercial vendors announcing support for Linux jumped dramatically. When the Linux bandwagon first began to roll, the trade press suggested, and many members of the Linux and open source communities feared, that many of the early announcements might turn out to be just hype, and much of the promised support would never be delivered. Less than a year later, those fears can be forgotten; a careful examination of the mainstream press uncovers an extraordinary picture of the change that is already well under way.

If you do a careful series of searches on one very focused topic in the Linux news, such as GUIs available for Linux, Linux deployments in business, or what a single vendor such as IBM, Compaq or Dell is doing to promote Linux, and browse through the articles published since early 1999, then you will realise that what's happening with Linux is massive.

Repeat that process on all the topics in the Linux news that you can think of, and then consider all your findings together; then you can appreciate the magnitude of what is happening and you soon realise that Linux has the potential to accomplish this David versus Goliath task.

Office applications and word processing

This section will examine the remarkable world of office software, concentrating on spreadsheets and word processors. There are basically three categories of office software you need to be aware of on Linux.

There are integrated office suites similar to Microsoft Office. There are stand-alone applications, word processors and spreadsheets. And there are tools that are neither word processors nor spreadsheets, but serve the same function.

These latter items characteristically come from the UNIX world rather than being ports of Windows applications; I include items like the TeX typesetting system and the LyX graphical front-end in this, because although LyX isn't a word processor you can use it to write letters or books and do the same sort of things you'd do with a word processor.

In the integrated office grouping, the two current leaders are StarOffice and ApplixWare. However, they will soon have to deal with by KOffice, the KDE integrated office suite, which at the time of writing is in beta testing, but looks like a creditable challenger. There is also SIAG Office, a distinctive open source office project that shows significant potential. Corel have promised to release Corel Office 2000 on Linux, but this is not yet available.

In the word processor grouping, there are a number of choices; WordPerfect 8 is, of course, the 'old man' of DOS-era word processors, and is available in a graphical version for Linux. There is also Maxwell, which was a commercial word processor that then became open source. In the spreadsheet group, we have WingZ, which was heralded as the best example in the spreadsheet marketplace, prior to Excel demolishing its Windows-based market, and SIAG, the pride and joy of SIAG Office, which can run on its own as a standalone spreadsheet, and is available as a stand-alone KDE version, KSIAG.

The TeX typesetting system is ubiquitous on UNIX, and a lot more accessible than the traditional UNIX typesetter, troff. With the LaTeX macro package, TeX allocates tools that make it comparatively straightforward to produce books, articles and letters using any text editor. You really don't need to learn all the control codes to type into your files, as there is a superb tool called LyX, and a KDE version, KLyX; these aren't WYSIWYG word processors, but a 'what you see is what you mean' word processor-like tool for creating and printing LaTeX files.

StarOffice

StarOffice is basically a clone of Microsoft Office 97. It's enormous, if you download it, running to 70Mb, and it has more functions than anybody could possibly ever use, but demands a lot of machine resources, typically 30–60Mb of memory. In practice, to run StarOffice 5.1 on an Intel-based Linux system, you need a minimum spec of a 166MHz processor and 64Mb of RAM.

The German company, Star Division, created StarOffice in 1984 to write a German language word processor. It expanded and developed ports into a number of operating systems, and was available on Linux in 1995 in a rather antiquated version, which bears no similarity to the efficient integrated suite presented today.

In August 1999, Star Division was bought out by Sun. Sun then announced some exciting developments. Star Division were formerly working on a port of StarOffice to Java, which is still being developed by Sun, whose forthcoming

StarPortal product is basically StarOffice for Java, designed to run on network computers. They're also releasing the source code to StarOffice under the Sun 'community source' licence. This is not true open source, as defined by Eric Raymond, insofar as Sun retain all rights to commercial derivatives: but it means that StarOffice will rapidly show up on non-Intel Linux platforms, such as PowerPC Linux and other flavours of free UNIX. It also means that StarOffice can be used for free, unless you're a major corporation deploying more than 500 copies of it in your organisation.

StarOffice comes as standard with many Linux distributions; you'll find it bundled free with SuSE Linux. If you don't have a copy, you can obtain it from Sun Microsystems at **www.stardivision.com**. (see Figure 5.2).

Figure 5.2   StarOffice

You can download it (but be warned, it is large and will take some time to download) or order a free CD.

Because StarOffice used to be shareware, it requires a registration number. Sun provide a generic licence, and say versions 5.2 and later won't need registering; meanwhile, you can use the following:

At the company name in the registration, enter: `Sun Free Download Version` and for the key enter `680A-0JH7-M60MVR-CQPD-147K`.

In use, StarOffice is noticeably similar to the earlier version of Microsoft Office. It provides a desktop, StarDesktop, that resembles the Windows 95 screen, right down to the Start button: the difference is that this is just the main window of the application, rather than a window manager. StarDesktop doesn't overwhelm the KDE applications; they run in their own windows, as usual.

StarOffice thankfully does not have any clone of Microsoft's talking paper-clip or those annoying little assistants. It does have a help feature that pops up hints and tips but this can easily be switched off. There are extensive online tutorials, and a huge reference manual for StarBASIC, StarOffice's built-in clone of Microsoft Visual Basic for Applications.

File format compatibility is *the* important problem for any office suite; we live in a world so dominated by Microsoft that their proprietary document for-mats are taken as the standard. StarOffice can take this in its stride; it has import and export filters for a complete range of formats, including HTML, Microsoft formats as far back as Word 6 and as far forward as Office 97, RTF, dBase, Lotus, earlier Star Division formats, and a range of image types. However, it does not behave with some of the UNIX environment's standards: LaTeX or troff documents, for example. While its filter set is lacking com-pared to ApplixWare or WordPerfect, it allows you to read and write Microsoft Office documents.

StarOffice is a very big, versatile package. Like Microsoft Office, it has functions that most of us can never even imagine a use for. Like Microsoft Office, too, StarOffice is a platform that you can write any dedicated business applications on; it incorporates the ability to produce HTML for a word processor. If you want to surf the Web, StarOffice includes a newsreader, mail tool and capable Web browser; it can even run JavaScript content and execute Java applets, if you tell it where your Java SDK (Solaris Development Kit) is installed. If you want to prepare drawings, there's a reasonable sketch package built in. For presentations, there's a clone of Microsoft PowerPoint.

StarOffice does not have quite the same range of examples and wizards as the Microsoft product but, on the other hand, the autopilots for creating new documents of specific types automate a lot of the time and effort, and more importantly it has the same feel. If you have no knowledge of Linux, and no knowledge of computers but wish to be able to type and use spreadsheets, then StarOffice is the application for you. It is basically Microsoft Office run-ning on a much more stable platform. It does almost everything you could want an office package to do and does so in a manner that will make Windows users feel comfortable.

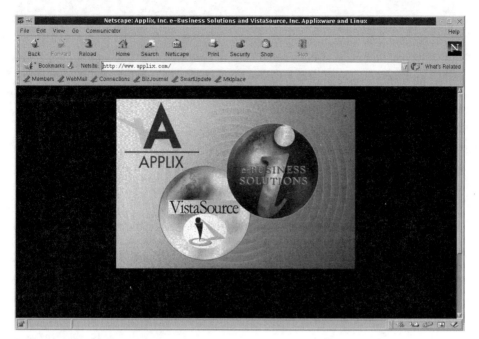

Figure 5.3   ApplixWare

ApplixWare

ApplixWare, from Applix Inc., is another big integrated office package. Unlike StarOffice, ApplixWare comes from the UNIX world (Figure 5.3). You can download a demo (limited) edition from **www.applix.com**. SuSE Office 99 comes bundled with ApplixWare 4.4.1.

Installation from the RPM files in the SuSE is very easy, but takes a lot of disk space; 250Mb for a single-language kit with the full online documentation and samples. There is no registration dialogue to fill in. In use, ApplixWare takes up much less memory than StarOffice: 8–16Mb in normal use. It will run happily on lower-end hardware, although a realistic minimum is a 70MHz machine with at least 32Mb of RAM and more if you plan on running GNOME or KDE at the same time.

When you start up ApplixWare, you get a small floating window with buttons to start up the various sub-applications: word, draw, sheet, mail and data, the SQL database query front-end. What you may not notice is the * (asterisk) menu, which gives you access to the full range of the ApplixWare suite, including Applix Presents, the obligatory PowerPoint clone, the HTML editor, and various customisation and macro dialogues.

ApplixWare does not look like Microsoft Office: it has a fairly traditional Motif look and feel, which might seem a little strange at first but is highly customisable. Motif is an open source GUI which used to be commercial. It has been somewhat left behind in development over the last two years while GNOME and KDE have forged ahead.

It is hard to criticise ApplixWare. Anything you could want to do in StarOffice you can also do in ApplixWare, albeit differently. The user interface incorporates pull-down menus and dialogue boxes rather than the cluttered Microsoft-clone style favoured by StarOffice. As with StarOffice, each application can embed objects that are actually documents created using another of the applications.

ApplixWare's file import and export filters are more extensive than those of StarOffice. Interleaf and FrameMaker are supported, along with WordPerfect and the usual Microsoft features, but there is no direct file exchange with StarOffice and vice versa. Unlike StarOffice, you need to explicitly import or export files; ApplixWare only works seamlessly on its own file formats, whereas StarOffice tries to deduce the type of a file and take appropriate action.

Applix Words feels simpler and less cluttered than StarOffice, but this is deceptive, because there are fewer toolbars and icons, but the functions are still there, under the menu tree. A particularly obvious way of exposing this hidden complexity is to look at the `Edit/Find and Replace` dialogue box. Embedded in this dialogue there is a powerful regular expression engine that also has the ability to parse styles. As with StarOffice and the other integrated suites and word processors, ApplixWare is able to cope with frames and do style-based mark-up; that is, to designate blocks of text as belonging to a certain style with set characteristics and layout.

On the database side, integration with ODBC-compatible databases and Informix, Ingres, Oracle, or Sybase is provided by Data. Unless you need to work with a database this probably will not mean much to you, but if you do, ApplixWare has extensive facilities to help you.

If you do not like the Microsoft styling of StarOffice, or do not need seamless interoperability with Microsoft applications; or if you need industrial-strength database integration or the ability to use your office package as a RAD tool, then ApplixWare is the tool for you.

KOffice

The potential of KOffice, which is not yet released but is currently in beta form, represents the future of office productivity suites.

Big commercial office suites like ApplixWare, StarOffice, Microsoft Office or Corel Office, are all feature-rich; but this is not necessarily a good thing. There are commercial pressures to release new versions of the software at regular intervals, even although there may be no customer demand: companies are in business to sell products, and will always try to persuade customers into purchasing new products by any means necessary. Marketing departments are commissioned to dream up new features, which may or may not be useful, or change user interfaces or file formats for whatever reason. Anyone who has been forced to upgrade a copy of Microsoft Word 6 because it cannot read or write more recent Word documents will appreciate how useful file formats can be to a marketing department.

Open source software has traditionally been recognised for bad user interface design because it was mostly written by programmers, for programmers: the developer's temptation was always to ignore the user interface and instead expose the workings of the program for fellow programmers to tinker with. SuSE Linux has now eliminated this with the introduction of YaST2, which provides a graphical interface that is very simple to understand and operate.

KOffice's home page can be found at **http://koffice.kde.org/** (Figure 5.4). KOffice represents a major revolution in the field of office suites. It consists of a group of teams working on sub-projects and developing the system using the open market technique that is the hallmark of successful open source projects. KOffice has no commercial pressures. The objective is not to maximise sales by forcing users to update their software regularly, or by adding obscure features that nobody wants: the goal is to produce a stable and reliable advanced integrated office environment as part of KDE, the K Desktop Environment. KOffice has been under development for about a year; it should be available with the release of KDE 2.0, probably in mid-2000, although you can download a developer's snapshot of the source code today.

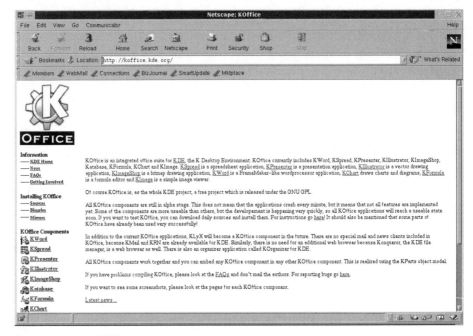

Figure 5.4 KOffice

While it is possible to use KOffice in its current state, it is probably a bad idea. Compiling it from scratch is not for the faint-hearted. Since it is still being developed it is still changing: it will continue to change until reaching its serviceable completion, subsequently the developers will concentrate on fixing any bugs that are left in it before a public release. So files you produce with a current snapshot may not be entirely compatible with a final version.

KOffice is an outstanding piece of software. At its heart is an ORB (object request broker), a server that lets programs request services from each other and over a network if required. It follows a document-centric model; you create a document using any of the KOffice tools and embed whatever data you want in it. If you are creating a word-processed document and want to incorporate a spreadsheet, you tell KWord to insert a sheet object and a live spreadsheet appears in a frame in your document. When you edit the sheet you are using the sheet application rather than the word processor.

Like Microsoft Office 2000, KOffice uses XML (extended markup language) as its common document format. XML is a subset of SGML (standard generalised markup language), a document description language which is to textual information pretty much what SQL is to databases. You may be familiar with HTML, the common language of the Web; HTML started life as a tiny subset of both XML and SGML.

Components of KOffice include KWord, a word processor that follows the model of FrameMaker, probably the best DTP package in the world, and which is already suitable for basic DTP work; and KSpread, a spreadsheet. KSpread, and soon the other KOffice tools, use the Python language for automation. This is a big improvement on overblown descendants of Basic, as Python is a powerful, modern object-oriented language.

Other components include KImage, an image viewer; KIllustrator, a vector graphics editor styled on Adobe Illustrator; KImageShop, a Photoshop-like bitmap editor; KPresenter, a PowerPoint-like presentation package; KFormula, a mathematical formula editor; KChart, for producing attractive output from spreadsheets; and KataBase, a relational database system.

It is also planned to make KLyX operate as a KOffice component, so that any other KOffice-type objects can be embedded in a KLyX document, and vice versa. At the time of writing, these tools are in various states of completion: some, such as KIllustrator and KPresenter, are very usable; others are usable but short on features and tend to crash (KWord); and some are barely present (KataBase). All the parts are present, and probably by mid-2000, KOffice will appear in Linux distributions everywhere. It is smaller in memory and disk space requirements, and more efficient, than other similar applications as it is not overloaded with extras that nobody uses. It has a far better scripting model, one based on a modern programming language that is easy to learn and extremely powerful. In view of the fact that it is not competing for market share against Microsoft Office or StarOffice, it does not have to handicap itself by imitating Microsoft's poor user interface; because it is not a commercial product like ApplixWare or Corel Office 2000, the developers can focus on whatever is useful rather than whatever sells extra copies. And because it is an open source project, like the Linux kernel, it promises to gather momentum suddenly and very visibly once it moves into beta testing. In 12 months time we may be looking back and wondering why on earth we ever bothered considering using a commercial office package.

SIAG Office

SIAG Office is a bit of a novelty. Standing for Scheme in a grid (Scheme is a dialect of the LISP programming language), it started out as a spreadsheeting tool for computer scientists, but has grown into a full-blown office suite. It is open source, but written principally by one developer, Ulric Eriksson. The complete suite consists of a spreadsheet (SIAG), a word processor (PW – Pathetic Writer), an animation program (Egon), a text editor (XedPlus), a file manager (Xfiler), and a postscript file previewer (Gvu).

SIAG Office was not written to make Windows users feel comfortable. The applications all use Emacs key bindings rather than the more familiar Windows or KDE key bindings, inherited from IBM's CUI standard by way of Windows 3. The programs all run as stand-alone applications; however, they integrate tightly, so that you can embed SIAG spreadsheets in PW documents, for example. Basic file import/export to Microsoft formats is supported, albeit with some loss of layout information; and there are far fewer obvious bells and whistles than in the larger office suites. For example, PW lacks Applix Words' extensive book indexing and cross-referencing tools, or StarOffice's plethora of style control settings.

SIAG Office has a lot of power where you would expect an open source project to have it: in its programmability. It is written around a Scheme interpreter, and all the commands and functions built into the various applications are exposed so that you can get at them by writing Scheme, or Tcl or Guile code. SIAG Office supports multiple application languages. As an example of its power, one of the example spreadsheets that comes with SIAG itself imple-

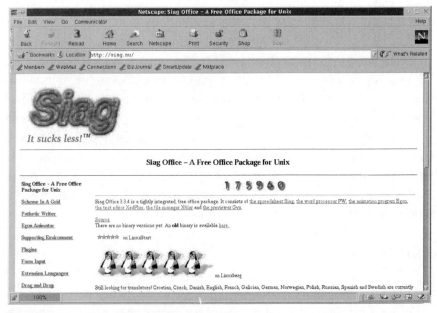

Figure 5.5 Siag Office's home page

ments a Web server! This is potentially a very powerful tool for automating Web-based forms, and SIAG Office will in general appeal to the more technically minded Linux user for its small size, extensibility and power.

There is also a port of the SIAG spreadsheet to the KDE user interface, which is nicer than the standard Xaw widget set that SIAG uses as standard. KSiag is currently the most solid, reliable spreadsheet for KDE, and if all you need is a spreadsheet it is the one to use, though this may change when the KOffice spreadsheet is reliable enough for day-to-day work. Siag Office is at **http://siag.nu/** (Figure 5.5).

Word processors

I first used WordPerfect many years ago, and at that time WordPerfect was simply the best word processor available. Time has gone by; WordPerfect Corporation lost out when Microsoft captured most of the PC user base with Windows and aggressively marketed Word. Then Corel bought WordPerfect, and then Corel got moved on to Linux. You can now download WordPerfect 8 for Linux for free, or buy a copy on CD, with masses of extra clipart, for not a lot of money. The Corel Linux Web site (Figure 5.6) is at **http://linux. corel.com/**.

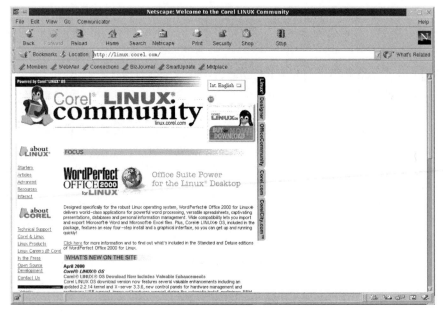

Figure 5.6 The Corel Linux Web site

WordPerfect has a much smaller disk and memory requirement than the integrated packages, taking about 6Mb of memory to run and 55Mb of disk space for a full install. It's also fairly economical in terms of screen space; it should be fine on smaller, older systems. Despite this, it isn't short on power features. In terms of word processing facilities, WordPerfect is the equal, or superior, of any of the integrated packages. In addition, it has some basic type-setting controls that StarOffice and ApplixWare lack, such as kerning and word/letter spacing controls, which make it fundamentally better suited to lightweight DTP (desktop publishing) work. And while it has confusing function key bindings, it also understands the CUI keystrokes such as `Alt-F` for the File menu, then `S` for Save. The list of file formats that WordPerfect 8 understands is huge, including items like Island Write and Interleaf, which will be of use to people coming from a UNIX text-processing environment, as well as Windows users.

On the minus side, WordPerfect cannot convert ApplixWare or StarOffice documents. To be fair, those two packages cannot interoperate with one another, either. And any attempts to import rich text format (RTF) or Word documents created with StarOffice into WordPerfect fail, possibly because RTF is not one file format but actually has about half a dozen different versions that Microsoft pins the one name on. If you don't need the spreadsheeting functions or you have a lower-end system, I would strongly recommend WordPerfect as your word processor.

LyX

LyX, pronounced 'licks', and the KDE version, KLyX, is not a word processor. It is a graphical front end for the LaTeX typesetting system; you can get it from **www.lyx.org** and see it in Figure 5.7. It behaves much like a word processor, and you use it for the same purpose, producing efficient printed documents.

Word processors all attempt to emulate typewriters, since when people began creating the first word processors, typewriters were what the users expected. You type a line of text and possibly underline bits of it, or insert markers into the text to indicate that the selected chunk is in a different typeface. LyX will not let you do that, because LyX is a front end for the TeX typesetting package. TeX is a compiler; you feed in a file containing instructions and text, and it emits PostScript, or an intermediate format, called DVI, containing the human-readable text formatted in accordance with those instructions. LaTeX (pronounced 'lay-tek') is a set of macros, TeX programs that give you a useful set of commands for formatting bits of a document;

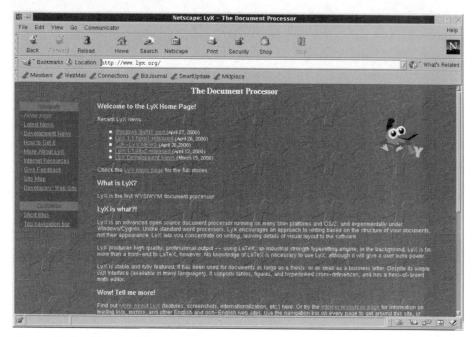

Figure 5.7 The LyX home page

if you type `\address{hello}` in a LaTeX document, TeX will format 'hello' using the address style defined by LaTeX.

TeX and LaTeX are loved by scientists because they produce very high-quality documents – typeset quality, in fact, with beautiful kerning and tracking, excellent hyphenation control and all the things that professional editors like to see in an academic paper. In fact, most refereed journals expect papers to be submitted to them in LaTeX or a related TeX format. But learning TeX macros is off-putting to someone who only wants to print off a quick letter, which is where LyX comes in.

LyX provides a word processor-like front end to LaTeX. You use it like a word processor and it produces LaTeX files that, when fed through TeX, produce beautiful typeset output. It shows you an impression of how your pages will look in print; it is a WYSIWYG environment, and instead of seeing raw text with embedded macros, you see text in whatever format it will appear on paper. KLyX differs from LyX only insofar as it provides a nicer KDE user interface, but takes up twice as much memory (roughly 6Mb instead of 3Mb) on an empty document window. It is hard to say how much disk space LyX or KLyX take up, because they both require a full LaTeX package to be installed. If you include all the supporting packages, fonts, DVI viewers and so forth, this can easily top the 50Mb mark.

LyX is especially good at cross-referencing, tables and indices, as well as mathematical formulae; it supports LaTeX to the maximum, and is full of features that will appeal to scientists or engineers producing documents. It is highly customisable, if you are willing to learn about TeX macros, and it is probably the ideal word processing solution for students, academics or engineers. It is, however, short on secretarial or office features, such as mail merge. If you want to do mail merge on TeX documents, the traditional way would be to write a perl or awk program to pull the appropriate information out of a database and insert it into a template file while feeding the latter through TeX.

Some secondary differences may annoy people who expect LyX to behave like a typewriter. Do you instinctively insert multiple spaces after a full stop? LyX (and TeX) will ignore them. TeX has its own ideas about how to space out text along a line, and a carriage return does not mean 'end of line': it means 'start a new paragraph'. Subtle differences, but they may take some getting used to if you are new to working with a typesetter.

The quality of output LyX produces is unsurpassed. If you want to grind out essays, papers, letters or a book, LyX is highly recommended.

Unfamiliar aspects of Linux – an historical perspective

Linux comes from the wonderful world of UNIX, and a lot of the common tools of the PC world do not have exact equivalents in UNIX. UNIX did not evolve big monolithic applications like word processors or spreadsheets; extremely powerful processes could be constructed out of simple tools, instead of needing one powerful program to do all the possible tasks relating to one problem domain.

For example, UNIX originally spread throughout Bell Labs in the early 1970s as a typesetting and word processing system. There was no word processing package; instead there was the troff typesetter; similar to TeX but more primitive and with a tendency towards obscure commands, it has been called 'the assembly language of desktop publishing' with good reason. The ed text editor came later, then vi, emacs and other tools.

These tools are still part of the Linux heritage, and you can find their up-to-date descendants such as groff, GNU troff, or vim and vi-IMproved in any Linux distribution. These programs do not have menus or graphical interfaces, and in many cases they have no online help, but they work, and they still do the job.

The fact that they're nearly 30 years old does not mean they're primitive or obsolete; it simply means that they're stable, not undergoing continuous development. Troff files created in 1975 remain readable today, which is something of a marvel when you compare this to the history of word processor file formats.

The moral of this story is that you don't need any of the products described in this section merely to do publication-quality typesetting or write a book using Linux. If you have the full SuSE Linux distribution installed on your computer, you will not need to add extra software to do something as basic as writing a letter. A second conclusion to draw from this is that if you learn about the inner parts of the Linux toolset, you will not be tempted to buy applications just because they promise to do something useful, because in most cases, everything you want to do can already be done using an obscure tool buried in /usr/bin. Because Linux is not a consumer operating system determined by the philosophy that consumers buy software, you may be surprised to discover how much it can do for you. The next section discusses features and functionality of SuSE Linux and answers some commonly asked questions.

Can it import a word document?

It seems that whenever I suggest a Linux word processor to a friend, they wait until I am finished describing all of the features and then ask, 'Can it import a Word document?' Like it or not, you are eventually going to receive an email attachment with the dreaded .doc extension. Regrettably, much personal and business communication is currently conducted on Windows machines through Excel spreadsheets, Word documents and other proprietary file formats.

Closed standards are unreliable, and essentially wrong. Proprietary file formats eradicate what we try to create: interoperability.

For the end user, the migration to a new application is painful. Many people will not use Linux because they are dependent on Microsoft Word.

Most people work in an assortment of environments and must be able to cope with other people's software choices. This is more than a matter of consideration; it is a matter of survival as well. The selection and quality of office suites available for any OS is one of the most critical aspects for adoption of that platform on the desktop.

Of all the companies striving to integrate itself with the Linux desktop, none have made as much progress as KOffice in the area of desktop integration. KDE and KOffice have built up an enormous head of steam and development is continuing at a very rapid pace. I use the KDE desktop and am anxiously awaiting the KDE team's next release, KDE2. KOffice will be included in KDE2 and will contain a full office suite including KWord, KSpread, KChart,

KImageShop and many others. KOffice will be able to do things never before seen in a Linux environment thanks to features like the KParts component embedding model and dcopserver, which enables communication between programs. Members of the KDE team are working on making filters. To keep abreast of what is happening in this development visit **http://koffice.kde.org/ filters/index.html** (Figure 5.8)

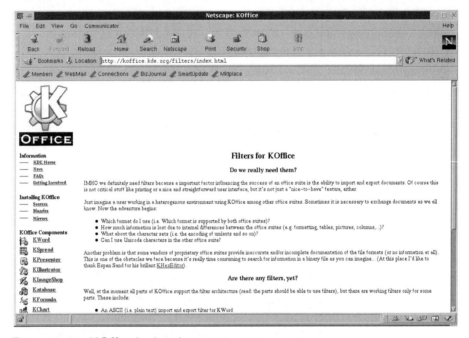

Figure 5.8   KOffice's development page

The way to judge the maturity of an office application is its ability to deal with non-native file formats. An application lacking this ability will be hindered in an office or home environment. This is an extremely important issue and critical to the adoption of Linux on the desktop.

Security

Security is an increasing worry for system and network administrators. Whether you just have one machine with your personal work on it, or a large network with dozens of servers and hundreds of clients, there is one common problem. Most Linux vendors install Linux so that you end up with a surplus of features and tools, often ignoring security considerations or not paying much attention to them. Unfortunately, security has a tendency to make the system harder to use; forgotten user-names and passwords are an increasing headache, and it is hard to teach users not to open email attachments from people they do not know. To make matters worse, most users simply don't place security as a high priority, and very few demand security features from their vendor.

SuSE Linux is making a real effort to produce a more secure distribution. It has a significant advantage

over most other large Linux vendors, as SuSE are located in Germany, whose government has taken an extremely pro-privacy stance in computing.

SuSE Linux has been writing and releasing a variety of software packages and scripts that enhance the overall safety and security of SuSE Linux. The first tool was a hardening script, which would lock down the system, disable various services and generally make the system a lot harder to break into. It ran as an interactive series of questions, or could be fed command line options, and made a log of what it did.

The SuSEauditdisk is an excellent tool. File integrity checking tools have existed for a long time; however, they all share one flaw. If an attacker is really skilled they can modify the Tripwire binaries. Say you keep them on a read-only floppy disk, and they can modify the system (i.e. the kernel) in such a way that Tripwire would report normal results. This is unlikely, but as soon as someone writes the code and it hits the Internet it would become widespread very quickly. The only truly secure way to check files is to boot from trusted media, that is, removable media that can preferably be set to read-only via hardware, such as a floppy disk, and stores the program and signatures on the same media. This is exactly what SuSEauditdisk is and does.

Another tool SuSE has made available is an ftp proxy (application level), which allows you to restrict the commands available to the user; you list which commands may be used in the configuration file. A potential use of this is for allowing access to an ftp server, since most ftp servers as of late have suffered root hacks, many due to the extraneous commands available that may not be needed. If you were to 'front' the server using this proxy you could easily disallow commands like `PUT`, and reduce the chances of an attacker misusing a command on the ftp server to gain additional access.

SuSE also has an advantage over American Linux vendors; in the USA the export of strong encryption software is heavily restricted and the RSA algorithm is patented, making use of it difficult. SuSE is based in Germany, and the German government is funding GnuPG development, an open source alternative to PGP.

SuSE ships with Apache mod-ssl (Apache with an add-on SSL package), Roxen, which is an open source, SSL-enabled Web server from Sweden, as well as several other similar packages.

Viruses

You probably heard about the Melissa virus. Various members of the great and the good of the IT community panicked, predicting the end of the Internet; some large financial institutions shut down their Internet email gateway in the hope of keeping it out.

Linux is not entirely immune to viruses. For example, a DOS boot sector virus that infests a dual-boot Linux/Windows machine can lie dormant while Linux is running, but whenever the machine reboots it may be activated and if it reboots on a flag day (a day when a virus is programmed to start) the virus may trash the system.

But there are some categories of virus that Linux is completely, or nearly completely, immune to. Many DOS or Macintosh viruses rely on appending copies of themselves to other uninfected executable files. Linux viruses have been written which do just that, but they have never been observed in operation. One reason for this is the Linux file access control system; you cannot write to a file that you do not have write permission for. This was inherited from UNIX, which started life as a minicomputer and mainframe operating system: many people could use each machine at the same time. Almost all of the programs on the system are therefore owned by the super-user, 'root' (or a user ID like 'news' or 'mail'), specifically to stop anyone from tampering with something that is rightfully the province of the mainframe's system administrator.

It follows that unless a virus has the good luck to get onto the system and be executed by a user with root privileges, it cannot append itself to most of the programs on the system. If it cannot append itself to programs, it cannot spread. And sensible system administrators do not just randomly run binaries downloaded off the net or a CD-ROM without taking precautions. Traditionally, system administrators built most of the software installed on their machine by hand, compiling and bug fixing if necessary; that is the UNIX way, and it is a good way of making sure the system is locked down tight.

In these days of home Linux and UNIX systems it is not something you can count on, but if you are able to follow the instructions in a readme file and compile the source yourself, you will be virtually immune to any nasty little infections that might lurk in pre-compiled binaries. If you cannot, well, try to spend as little time as possible logged on as 'root' rather than under your own, non-privileged username.

A secondary mechanism used by some Mac and Windows viruses is that they try to infect running programs in memory, piggy-back onto them, and copy themselves to other running programs. The UNIX virtual memory system blocks this efficiently; it ensures that each running process has its own distinct memory space and can neither see nor write to any other program's memory. This is one reason why Linux is so much more stable than MacOS or Windows.

And now for the third, and probably the most important, reason why Linux is not easy prey for viruses like Melissa: it is a true multi-user system that defines variable levels of trust and is built from the bottom up with security in mind, and it draws a clear line between applications and the operating system.

Microsoft are famous for claiming that a Web browser is an integral part of their operating system; that, after all, is what the recent anti-trust trial was supposedly all about. Microsoft's Windows started off as a graphical shell on top of MS-DOS, itself a clone of CP/M. CP/M was an unpretentious single-user operating system with no security to speak of, when only one person can use a computer at a time, and only one program runs at a time. Twenty years later things were different. Microsoft had slowly evolved into a networking, multitasking, GUI, virtual memory situation where the user would not always be in control, or aware, of all the processes going on in their machine. And nowhere prior to

Did you know that...?

Graphical user interface

A GUI is a graphical representation of a normal desktop. Whereas you lay different papers onto a normal desktop, here these 'papers' are called windows. You can put as many of these windows on your desktop as you like. Each individual process runs in a separate window. A GUI is normally controlled via a mouse, trackball or something similar. Some well-known GUIs are the X Window System, Apple Macintosh System 7, Digital Research GEM and MS-Windows.

Windows NT did anyone sit down and say, 'We have in effect built a multi-user system! Why don't we think about implementing a security policy?'

On the contrary: Microsoft completely ignored multi-user context and security issues. In effect, all users and programs have root privileges. NT goes some way to redress the issue, which is one reason viruses are less common on Windows NT. Meanwhile, all sorts of automation features were built into their applications. Automation, in the form of Visual Basic interpreters with access to inter-process communication, via OLE/ActiveX, is a wonderful tool. Automation without a security policy is, however, a virus-writer's dream.

One of the much-trumpeted design characteristics of Java was that the Java virtual machine provided a means of security for Java programs. Standard ActiveX and VBA on Windows 98 has no such protection mechanism, which is why a Word document, delivered via email and opened by clicking on an attachment's icon, was allowed to rifle through a private address book, maintained by a different application, and send email to other people without the user even being aware of it.

There are many applications on Linux that have built-in automation languages. However, unless you deliberately set out to compromise your system's security policy and modify some start-up command files, there is no way that merely opening a file in vim will trigger the execution of scripting commands hidden inside it. And this pattern is repeated across almost all Linux sub-systems. This does not mean that Linux is invulnerable. A particular point of vulnerability is the Internet; not from random viruses, but from bad people who want to get access to your machine's resources or network connection from outside.

If you provide network services like mail and news, programmers can find out open ports, using tools called port scanners, and attempt to feed bogus data to the servers in the hope of crashing them and making them execute arbitrary commands.

You must be careful about blocking unused services and tracking changes in system files. Tripwire is an indispensable tool for monitoring these files; see **http://www.tripwire.com/** for details (Figure 5.9). Most of the loopholes exploited by crackers get blocked fairly rapidly, but if you run an old or out-of-date system you may be vulnerable.

One important law of security is that 'security through obscurity' does not work. That is, if you make some sort of software product and find it has a security hole, trying to preserve security by stifling discussion of it simply won't work; sooner or later some curious cracker will figure out it exists, and when that happens all the crackers will soon know but your users will still be in the dark. The best antidote to security holes is a security fix. Linux is in general very good about this sort of thing; security holes are yelled about and patches distributed within hours or days of their discovery. So you may get the impression that Linux has more security problems than, say, Windows, because you hear more about them: but in reality, what is happening is the security problems are being fixed instead of being ignored.

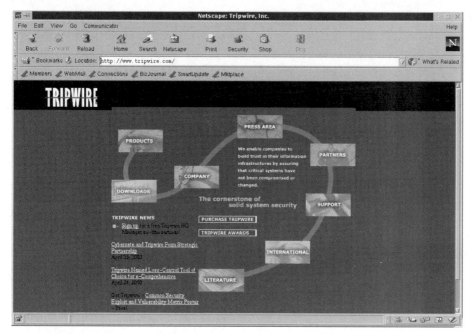

Figure 5.9 Tripwire: an indispensable tool

In contrast, when a bug in the Windows 95 TCP/IP stack emerged that allowed anyone with a simple program to send the machine a 'ping of death' that would crash it, it took Microsoft weeks to issue a patch and even now many users are unaware that their systems are vulnerable. Why would Microsoft want to cause unnecessary terror among their users?

Even if you only run a dial-up connection, you may be vulnerable to attack by outsiders. The worst culprits are spammers, a particularly unpleasant species who will exploit your unsecured mail or news server to send junk advertisements to other people. This is a real nuisance if it happens to you; it clogs up your network connection, possibly causing you to stay online much longer than you wanted to, and it wastes time and money. In fact, it is theft at your expense. The important points to note here are that a dial-up system should (a) not accept news postings from any other

---

Did you know that...?

Email

The means of transporting mail electronically between registered users via a network. Similar to normal mail (which is often referred to as 'snail mail'), the email address has to be entered as `sender@sender's-domain.country` to `recipient@recipient's-domain.country`. Email lets you send not only text, but also attached documents and pictures. Email has many advantages: it is cheap and usually reaches its destination within minutes.

machines, and (b) not relay email from one foreign domain to another. It should originate or receive mail, but not act as a post office: that is your ISP's job.

To stop spammers from posting news, you may want to investigate TCP wrappers, a tool for restricting who can access your network servers. Mail is more of a headache, as it depends what mail transport system you use; Sendmail users, which in practice means most people, should look at Sendmail at **www2.sendmail.com** (Figure 5.10).

Figure 5.10   The Sendmail site

Some particularly skilled crackers write automatic tools that attempt to propagate themselves from one machine to another. Mostly these tools (called worms) rely on exploiting one or two common security loopholes; and most do not work. The big exception was the Great Internet Worm of 1988. The worm attacked some known 'back doors' on DEC's VMS operating system and on Sun's then-current version of SunOS, a UNIX system. Due to a bug in the worm, it propagated uncontrollably, reinfecting already infected computers until they ground to a standstill; at its worst it affected 60 per cent of the Internet, which then hosted a mere 50,000 or so machines.

No Linux-specific worm has been confirmed, but as Linux continues to spread you can bet that some idiot will try to write one, which is part of the reason it pays to keep abreast on security issues. Incidentally, the back doors that RTM's worm exploited were slammed very hard indeed, immediately afterwards!

A must-have in any Linux installation is one of the widely available open source scanning applications. A security scanner lets a network administrator scan the network for possible signs of intrusion or other malicious damage. Some of these scanning tools, such as Nessus at **www.nessus.org**, can even look for security vulnerabilities across multiple operating systems. That way, Linux administrators can scan their entire networks, rather than just their Linux nodes, all at once (Figure 5.11).

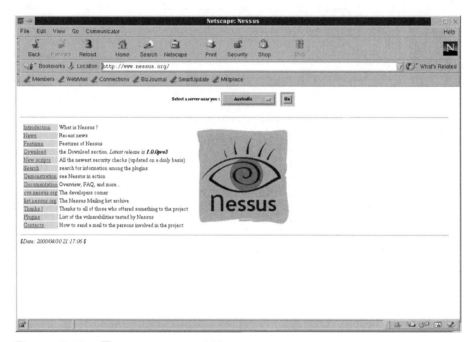

Figure 5.11   The scanning tool Nessus

Finally, the best way to ensure safety in the Linux world is to take the time necessary to understand the operating system. Many Windows users have criticised Linux in this regard, saying the operating system is much harder to use than Microsoft's software. In reality, building a really secure NT server requires as much in-depth knowledge of the operating system as it would under Linux.

There is no getting around it: security means becoming intimately familiar with your operating systems of choice, or at least hiring people who are.

Once you know more about Linux, you will be able to move away more comfortably from default installations. That can be a huge security gain, because removing unwanted or unneeded applications and processes from

Did you know that...?

Network File System (NFS)

This is a protocol to access file systems of networked machines. On the server side the configuration `file/etc/exports` determines which machines may access which directory trees on the server. The client may then 'mount' these directories in his own directory tree.

your Linux server always means closing a door on a potential security hazard. Indeed, understanding which network services are enabled by default is the key to securing any network host. In addition to exposing too much network information through DNS, other services, remote procedure calls in particular, can expose critical information about your hosts that you may not want outsiders to know. As a rule, if you do not need a network service, disable it or, better still, remove it from your hosts.

Learning more about Linux also means that you will become more familiar with the security options already inherent in Linux, such as its ability to be converted easily into an IP firewall or proxy server.

In a practical sense, Linux's open source foundation also provides another security benefit. Realistically, few companies can rigorously review every line of source code in an operating system to locate security weaknesses. Just as the open collaborative development model makes Linux such a success, the same effect lets all Linux users benefit from the security reviews of programmers throughout the world. Because so many pairs of eyes have examined parts of the Linux source code, there is a far greater chance that security flaws will be found and fixed.

The bottom line is that open source software represents a few more unknowns than traditional commercial software but, with a little time and effort, you can turn those unknowns into advantages to keep your network safer than ever.

Summary

Linux does not get viruses; some genius may figure out how to infect it successfully, but I'm not holding my breath. Linux is, however, vulnerable to different kinds of attack: these are most critical if you run a server which is connected to the Internet all the time, but they can still affect dial-up users and a particular problem is spammers grabbing mail and news access. The solution is to know how the Linux system security works, and attempt to keep abreast of current developments and security alerts.

Emulators

Having the ideal emulator for another operating system and, if possible, for other architectures is many computer users' dream. What makes them so desirable is they can run in a window of your favourite operating system and can play all your favourite games, and you can use them to do some real work as well.

Linux has emulators for just about every operating system under the sun. The task of a software emulator is to provide an environment in which programs written for another system can run. Computers, being general purpose information processors, are all functionally equivalent at a very deep level. You might think that an emulator will almost always run much more slowly than the original hardware, and you would be right; but given that in the computing industry there is a doubling of performance every 18 months or so, it should also come as no surprise to learn that a modern PC or Mac running an emulator will outperform any computer which is over four years old.

In this section I will try to give you some understanding of the wonderful world of emulators and what the future will hold for them.

DOS emulator

First there is the old standby, the DOS emulator. Linux has a very good DOS emulator that allows an Intel-based computer to generate a virtual 8086 (or virtual 386) environment in which you can boot a copy of DOS. The main emulation tool, DOSEMU (**www.dosemu.org/**) (Figure 5.12) has been around for years and will run most DOS applications.

If you are running Linux on a Mac or SPARC or Alpha box instead of a PC, there is an alternative in the form of Bochs at **www.bochs.com.** (Figure 5.13)

Bochs does not rely on forcing your PC to generate a virtual 86 session; instead it provides a complete emulation of an Intel 80386 CPU in software – slow, but good enough to boot DOS (or Windows NT, for that matter). Bochs is commercial software – but with full source code available for 30-day evaluation.

There is also the very interesting open source WINE project at **www.winehq.com** (Figure 5.14).

WINE is one of those self-referential acronyms, short for 'WINE is not an emulator'. The goal of the WINE project is to allow any Windows application to run transparently on Linux, by providing a full array of services that replicate the Windows environment, at least as far as an application sees it. With WINE support, Linux on Intel-based hardware can load and directly execute Windows applications. Most Windows 3.1 programs that don't directly conflict with the underlying hardware run very well on WINE; simpler Windows 95 applications also run, although support for the Win32 API's is partial at present.

There's a second freeware Windows emulation project on Linux; TWIN, which was originally a commercial project by Willows Software. It is at **www.willows. com** (Figure 5.15).

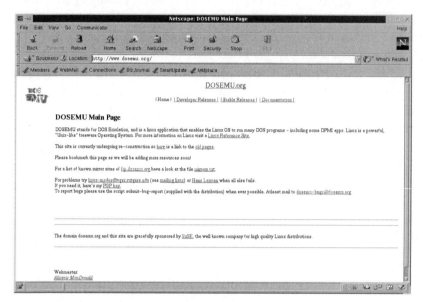

Figure 5.12   DOS emulation page

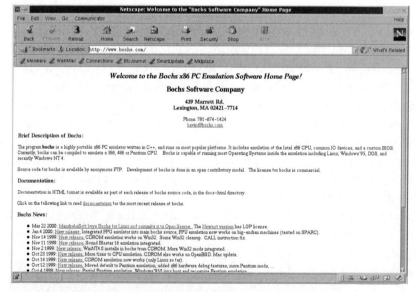

Figure 5.13   Bochs Emulation Software home page

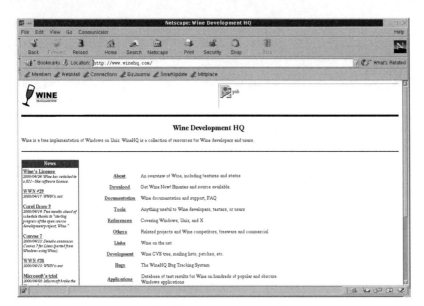

Figure 5.14   The WINE home page

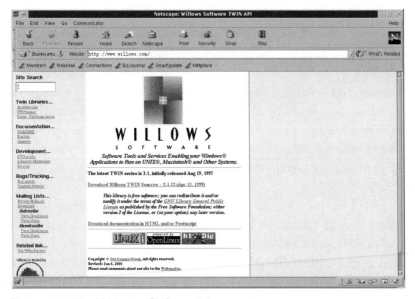

Figure 5.15   Willows Software home page

TWIN is now open source and work is underway to merge relevant parts of the TWIN source code base with WINE, thus making the TWINE project. Visit it at **www.codeweavers.com/twine/** (Figure 5.16).

Figure 5.16 TWINE project

VMware

There is another PC emulation environment you need to know about: VMware. VMware enables you to run Windows 98 or NT as an application under Linux or vice versa by handling context switching between OSs. VMware is commercial and you have to pay for it, though it is worth every penny, but you can find a 30-day limited demo at **www.vmware.com** or in a copy of the SuSE 6.4 distribution (Figure 5.17).

VMware is not just an emulator. It is a complete virtual machine 'built' on the underlying layer of hardware and the existing operating system. It does not take control of your keyboard, mouse and video; you can run it in full-screen mode as well as in a window. This, however, requires some modifications to get everything to act as usual. The virtual machine runs on top of the existing OS, using its devices to access the underlying hardware. The great advantage of this is that you can have up to four virtual network adapters on your virtual machine, and have them all bound to the network, which uses the hosting OS as the gateway.

Figure 5.17 VMware

You are not tied to one operating system. Just as I tried Windows NT on Linux, I tried Linux on Windows NT; there is a version of VMware for Windows NT too. Not only can you run Microsoft's operating systems or Linux under VMware, you can use BSD as well, or BeOS, plain DOS, virtually everything that is made for the x86 platform. You can run two at the same time, if you wish. However, since it takes at least 64Mb of additional RAM for each new virtual machine, not to mention the CPU load, your machine will become slower with each application.

There is much to gain in using virtual machines. If you write code or work at a helpdesk you can develop it on your 'real' machine and test the software on the virtual one. If it

Did you know that...?

Central Processing Unit (CPU)

Intel x86 processors can be run in many different modes. Here, we want to distinguish between two of them. Real mode is the 'original' mode using a segmented memory protocol. This is slow, antiquated and limited to 16-bit software. Protected mode (available from 386 onwards) has a linear memory. Only this mode uses the full power of the CPU. Linux runs only in protected mode. At the time of writing, Linux exists for the following processor architectures: Intel x86, DEC alpha, Motorola m68k, Sparc, PowerPC, MIPS and ARM.

crashes, all you have to do is to restart the virtual machine, and the underlying OS will be unaffected by the crash of the one running in the VM. The disk images have the ability to undo changes made in the last session. So if you do something weird to the file system on the disk images, you can repair it easily. You can use real hard disk partitions instead of disk images.

If you run one operating system but need software that runs on another OS, there is chance for you to get the best of both worlds.

VMware isn't free; the Windows version without the SuSE Linux image CD costs £200, and £207 including it. If you are a student, you pay around £70–£75. Prices for the Linux platform are the same. If you want, you can download a demo version, which will allow you to play with it for a limited time. You can find the demo at **www.vmware.com/download/ download_linux_pre.html** for Linux, and at **www.vmware.com/download/ download_win_pre.html** for Windows (Figures 5.18 and 5.19).

Keep in mind that you need at least a Celeron and 128Mb of memory if you want it to run VMware smoothly. More CPU power and RAM will not hurt. If you have two CPUs and you will get two virtual machines, each on its own CPU.

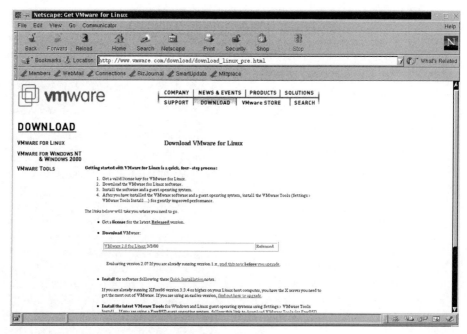

Figure 5.18   Download VMware for Linux

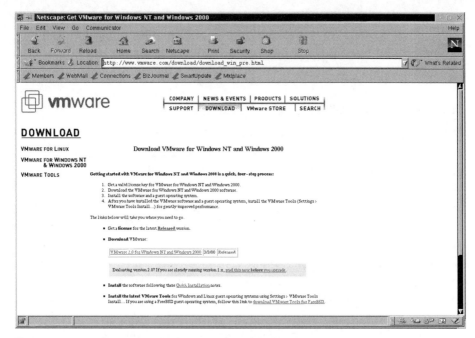

Figure 5.19   Download VMware for Windows

What is the market for VMware?

There are many market targets that are suitable for VMware: people who need Windows productivity applications on Linux (office, mail, browsers) because they can run Windows programs without the need to reboot the computer; developers who write and test software as well as people who provide tech support, because they can have multiple platforms to work on and test various configurations at the same time; people who develop Web content and Web sites, because they can use different browsers on different platforms to preview the content they're working on.

VMware can change the way people think about their PC and operating system. Today, there is a 1:1 mapping between your hardware, the OS you run and the applications you can run: for example, on a PC running a Windows operating system, you can run only Windows NT and/or Windows-compatible applications; on a Linux PC you can run only Linux-compatible applications, and so on.

And there is no way to concurrently run applications for Windows NT and Linux on the same PC, natively. As a result, you are limited in what you can do: software testing, installs and upgrades are tedious and time-consuming. Operating system or application crashes have a high impact and bring down the PC. There is a limit in the applications you can run. With VMware, you can now do much more: install software or test upgrades in a safe environment without impact on your working world. A crash within a virtual machine is limited to that environment and will not affect the rest of the PC. Run the applications you need, regardless of the OS requirement.

Comparing Bochs and WINE projects with VMware

WINE allows some unmodified Windows 3.1, 9x and NT binaries to run on Intel PCs under Linux and other x86 UNIX-like operating systems. WINE is an implementation of the Windows 3.x and Win32 APIs on top of X and Unix. One advantage of WINE is that it does not require a separate Microsoft operating system to run applications. WINE also provides relatively good performance as application code runs natively on the underlying hardware. Individual Windows applications may or may not be supported by WINE. WINE is an alternative implementation of the Win32 API while VMware is a virtual machine monitor. VMware allows multiple operating systems to run by multiplexing them onto the underlying hardware. VMware requires a Microsoft operating system to run Windows applications and provides very high levels of application compatibility. VMware also provides advanced capabilities such as isolation and encapsulation that WINE does not provide.

Bochs is an emulator: it runs entirely at user level and emulates all of the different devices and CPU instructions. VMware is a virtual machine monitor (not an emulator or simulator) and as such will take advantage of the underlying hardware to execute instructions and have much better performance. Also, Bochs is not feature-complete; at the time of writing, networking and some other features were still being worked on.

How secure is VMware?

Is it possible to break in from the cracked virtual box to the real operating system?

The virtual machine is like another computer on the same network. If you have the virtual machine VM1 running on top of the host H1, it is like having two machines, VM1 and H1, on the same LAN. As such, any security violation that can be done between two machines on the same LAN can be done between VM1 and H1 (through networking protocols). From VMware's perspective, the memory and disk are completely isolated. One cannot get to read and/or corrupt data on H1 through the VM1. If you decide not to have networking on VM1, disable the Ethernet interface through the settings panel, and it will be totally isolated from the rest of the world. There is a variety of other networking settings that you could apply to VM1 and H1: attach H1 to VM1 through a VPN (virtual private network) and VM1 to the world on the Internet, set one up as a firewall and use IP masquerading for the other one, and so on. You can therefore do much more with a PC when using VMware.

With VMware you can not only boot to multiple operating systems, but also run them simultaneously. You can run Windows 98, Linux and Windows 2000 on the same machine all at the same time, with each OS isolated so as not to affect the others.

VMware is paving the way to a higher level of computing with their Virtual Platform software. VMware gives users an innovative solution to platform incompatibility that offers flexibility and superior performance.

How does VMware work?

VMware Virtual Platform is a thin software layer that permits multiple operating systems to run simultaneously, using the same hardware resources. This is made possible by transparently multiplexing all hardware resources into multiple virtual machines. Each virtual machine has a unique network address and resembles the underlying machine. VMware is installed on a host OS (either Linux or Windows NT). Once installed, various guest OSs can be loaded and run concurrently with the host OS.

Although the ability to concurrently run multiple OSs on the same machine is its most advertised feature, that is certainly not all it does. The features of VMware are as follows:

1. It can encapsulate a virtual machine and enable it to be moved freely around a different physical machine.

2. It provides each virtual machine with fault isolation and containment capabilities, meaning that if an application crashes or data corruption occurs in a given virtual machine this will not affect data or applications outside of that virtual machine.

3. Developers can use a single machine to write and test applications for multiple target environments.

4. Organisations can efficiently install new or upgraded versions of operating systems or applications throughout their project, while keeping their current operating system and applications intact.

5. All users can work with confidence because they know any changes they make to a system can be undone with just a click of a mouse button.

6. Multiple operating systems can be run simultaneously in separate virtual machines on a standard PC.

7. Virtual machine sessions can be run on the Windows NT desktop or run in full-screen mode; other virtual machines continue to run in the background.

8. You can use a key to switch between virtual machines.

9. Operating systems already installed on a multi-boot computer will run without reconfiguring.

10. You can install a virtual machine without repartitioning your disks.

11. You can share files and applications among virtual machines using a virtual network within a PC.

12. You can run client/server, Microsoft BackOffice, or Web applications between virtual machines on the same PC.

13. VMware Virtual Platform uses all the processor components, consequently eliminating the overhead typically associated with PC emulators.

Power users are the ones who will get the most out of VMware. They will find it very convenient to run additional instances of Windows NT or other OSs. VMware for Windows NT installs as any standard application would.

Windows NT power users will get the following benefits. It is possible to:

1. Develop and test applications simultaneously for multiple target environments.

2. Evaluate beta releases without endangering the host OS.

3. Run real MS-DOS, extensions, and applications.

4. Add new OSs without disk repartitioning.

5. Network virtual environments and share files and devices.

6. Undo any changes made in a user session to recover from problems, including registry corruption or viruses.

7. Run legacy applications while simultaneously running the latest operating systems and applications.

8. Run Linux with concurrent access to Windows NT and any other Windows applications.

These are some of the incredible features offered by this revolutionary software, but what kind of machine does it take to run it? The requirements for running VMware are unremarkable.

Hardware requirements for VMware are:

1. Standard PC with Intel Pentium or compatible processor (Pentium II or compatible recommended).

2. Minimum 64Mb memory (96Mb recommended).

3. 3Mb disk space for basic install.

4. At least 500Mb free disk space recommended for each guest operating system and application.

Rarely do you find a product that makes you think that this is how the future of computing will evolve, but VMware is possibly that. The technology behind VMware software is nothing short of remarkable, enabling a user to run a second operating system in a virtual environment in Linux.

With the rapid advance of mobile code on the Internet, having a virtual machine that runs within a browser and implements all code before it hits the client machine will prevent many nasty surprises. Sun has attempted this with Java's sandbox architecture, but VMware does not require a specific language or operating system.

This technology also could be used in everything from microwaves to cars, selecting embedded systems to allow software written for Windows to run on top of real-time operating systems.

VMware acts as a layer between the hardware and the operating system. VMware stress that the product is not an emulator, but it most certainly looks like one to me.

VMware abstracts the hardware and intercepts most signals going to the CPU. Products such as the open source WINE, in contrast, translate the Win32 APIs into Linux-compatible calls, allowing Linux to run Windows applications. Each method has advantages: translation can be faster, but emulation offers a higher level of compatibility.

Ease of installation

VMware for Linux installs effortlessly on a 233MHz Pentium PC running Linux. To configure the machine, I simply allocated memory and hard disk space to the virtual machine, where I installed Windows NT 4.0 along with Service Pack 4. VMware runs any Windows operating system and applications without partitioning or rebooting. VMware's emulation was evident in the virtual machines: all that NT saw for networking was the Advanced Micro Devices Ethernet network interface card.

VMware site

The Linux community has created a FreeMWare site (check out **www. freemware.org**), for all-free virtual computing for Linux. It is still far from being usable but it is one to keep your eye on (Figure 5.20).

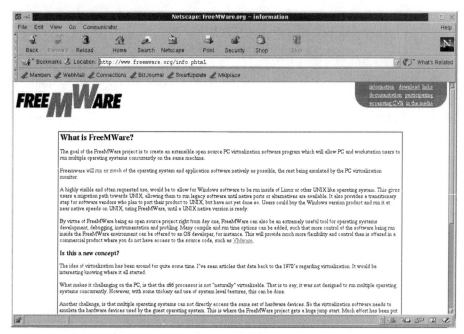

Figure 5.20   The Linux community's FreeMWare site

Linux on laptops

The requirements for my laptop are simple: it must be Linux-compatible. I make my living travelling the world and I rely on my laptop to survive, so I am not going to be satisfied with a computer that only runs Windows. I use an IBM ThinkPad and operate with two exchangeable hard disks; one dedicated to Linux and the second a dual boot system, which allows me to run both Linux and Windows. For partitioning my Linux/Windows hard disk I use a wonderful piece of software from PowerQuest called Partition Magic. This masterpiece of software provides the benefits of partitioning to anyone in a fast and trouble-free manner. The PowerQuest Web site is at **www. powerquest.com** (Figure 5.21).

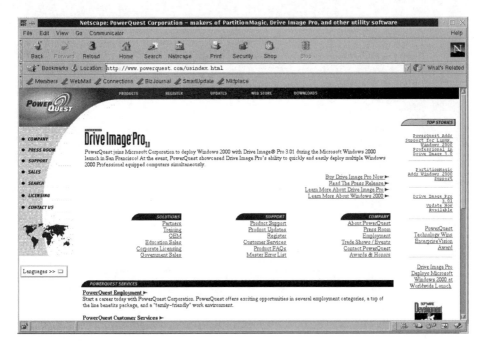

Figure 5.21   The PowerQuest site

PowerQuest has some excellent products and SecondChance is a program that I believe should be installed with every Windows operating system. Have you ever changed a system setting and found that it slowed down your computer's performance, or downloaded a file that caused problems for your system? Perhaps you have unsuccessfully tried to get rid of a partially installed program.

SecondChance provides a simple, reliable, convenient way to undo the effects caused by a software system crash, application conflict or user error. It can return your computer to an earlier point in time, called a checkpoint, when it was working to your satisfaction. You just select the checkpoint you want to return to, click a button, and SecondChance restores your computer to that checkpoint.

As computer systems become more complicated, with being able to add new software and download files from the Internet, the probability that a user's computer will be affected by unstable software, system changes, deleted data, system failure or other problems drastically increases. The ability to return your computer to an earlier position when it worked properly is becoming increasingly important for every computer user. SecondChance could save every computer user time and trouble.See **www.powerquest.com/secondchance/index.html** and Figure 5.22.

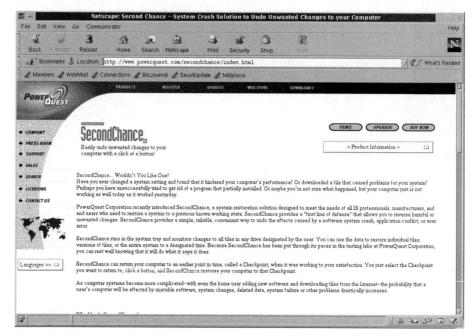

Figure 5.22 The SecondChance site

Laptops, especially brand new ones, are notorious for causing headaches to users of the Linux-based operating system. Laptop manufacturers delight in packing their machines with new chips and devices whose design seems to change by the hour. Linux programmers are often one or two steps behind those manufacturers in the struggle to write code that allows Linux to make use of such hardware. Indeed, one of the main difficulties for the Linux-based operating system is its lack of support for brand new hardware. The problem is that it is difficult for Linux programmers to gain access to the hardware specifications that they need in order to write code which will work with that hardware. This, in turn, is because many hardware manufacturers, especially those who aim at the consumer marketplace, consider the Linux market too small to warrant accommodating.

In some areas, considerable progress has been made over the last six months. The leading makers of 3D video chips are racing to ensure that their most recent developments work with Linux; they are increasingly aware that the game players who tend to buy the fastest 3D chips are also often Linux programmers.

The biggest problem for anyone installing Linux is any modem carrying the word 'WinModem'. WinPrinters are also a problem. In fact WinAnything will cause problems. The new kernel may eliminate these problems; but more on that later.

The term WinModem is a trademark owned by 3Com Corp., which itself owns US Robotics, one of the world's leading modem manufacturers. WinModem is used to describe a class of products, sometimes called 'software modems', in which key telecommunication functions that were once handled by hardware have been moved into the software domain.

For this software to work properly, your computer needs to be running Windows. WinModems are popular with both desktop and laptop makers because they are cheaper than hardware modems, and therefore lower the over-all cost of a computer. They also save valuable space, a vital factor for laptop makers. Most machines that have a built-in modem have a WinModem and as far as Linux is concerned it is a cheap ineffective device.

It is no fun to buy a new laptop and then discover that, no matter how good a programmer you are, you simply cannot get the built-in modem to work with Linux. There are workarounds, external modems or network cards that can be plugged in to PCMCIA slots or otherwise connected, but who wants to use up a valuable PCMCIA slot or lug around an external modem when your computer already has one built in?

For Linux users, the fact that most Sony Vaio laptops come with modems that do not require Windows has been enough to encourage a wave of Vaio buying. But Sony offers no universal remedy, because some of their latest models of Vaio now include WinModems.

Just attempting to discover which modem is inside a laptop can be a major irritation. Not only is there a bewildering abundance of laptops on the market, but there is no modem consistency within a particular brand. Some IBM ThinkPads, for example, use a particular type of WinModem made by Lucent. But other models employ IBM's own patented MWave technology, a complex combination of sound and modem features.

The Linux community is currently pursuing an independent strategy to address the problem of WinModems. In classic fashion, scores of programmers have busied themselves with attempts to write their own 'drivers', swatches of code that allow a particular operating system to communicate with a particular piece of hardware, with or without the help of the hardware manufacturer.

Unfortunately the Linux community does not have the necessary technical documents and the problem for prospective WinModem users is getting the manufacturers to release drivers designed for Linux. Ideally, Linux program-mers would prefer that the source code to the drivers be released to the general public and then it could be included in the Linux kernel. Even if the source code were never to be released, most programmers would be happy just to get drivers that worked with Linux.

IBM gets fairly high marks from programmers for its record of co-operation with the Linux community. Their high-performance Netfinity servers will run Linux and they are certainly encouraging the various suppliers they work with to progress to provide capacity for Linux support.

The most dedicated resources on Linux regarding laptops can be found at Linux on Laptops at **www.cs.utexas.edu/users/kharker/linux-laptop** (Figure 5.23). This is the ultimate site for information on how to get Linux to run on any laptop. You will find at this site hundreds of detailed accounts of how people managed to get Linux running on a particular laptop. And there is always the possibility that in the future, hardware advancements will make current WinModem worries obsolete.

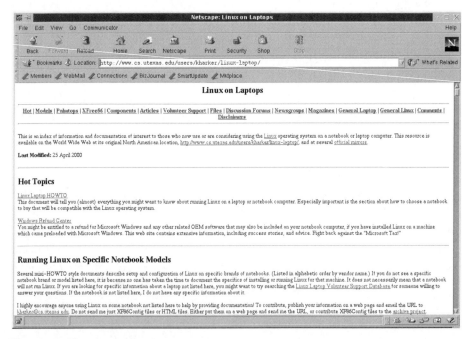

Figure 5.23   Linux on Laptops

Linus Torvalds recently declared his belief that future hardware design would solve many of today's incompatibility problems. I predict that in the near future the end user will be able to buy standard compliant devices that will work on Linux, on PC, on Mac and potentially in the future on palm-type devices. A future in which everything 'just works' is the goal that the Linux community is working towards.

Do not think you have to buy a new laptop if you want to have a mobile Linux system. Apart from the usual WinModem problems, you could be running Linux on an old laptop and get a few more productive years out of a laptop that might not be fast enough any more under Windows.

In many ways Linux is much more suitable for portable operation than Windows. Linux seems to be more reliable coming out of suspend mode; Windows 98 will hang on my laptop if I open the lid without either reconnecting the Ethernet or unplugging the network card. Linux will not, and will happily let me change networks without rebooting, or even logging out. My desktop machines are also reliable: they stay up for months at a time, shutting down only for hardware upgrades and power failures. Linux has always used the HALT instruction when the CPU is idle, rather than sitting in a tight loop wasting power as Windows does. The CVS version-control system is wonderful for synchronising my working files between work, home and the laptop. So is rsync, for that matter.

Using the X Window System, I can log in on my laptop from my desktop machine and do anything on it that I could from the keyboard. Any windows I had open will still be there after I have taken the machine home, used it over the weekend, and come back to the office on Monday. Because Linux, unlike NT, is a real multi-user OS, I do not have to log out in order to perform system administration tasks or to switch between my work and home roles.

Linux's excellent multi-tasking lets me run both a Web server and a browser without a noticeable performance effect. I can use Netscape and Apache for presentations, and still have plenty of computing capacity left. People tend to like either laptops or desktops. I prefer laptops. I feel very comfortable using Linux and its raw unbridled computing power. I don't claim to be a laptop expert, I just had the opportunity to install SuSE Linux two years ago on an IBM ThinkPad 380XD and I had a problem getting it to recognise the PCMCIA card. This was on a Saturday morning and I sent off a plea for help to a Linux help group on the Web. Within an hour I had over 70 replies to my problem. I experienced the worldwide support and help available for Linux, which is given voluntarily by the Linux community, and I was smitten. I had my PCMCIA card operational and within 20 minutes was surfing the Web.

Due to a lack of support by some hardware manufacturers, not every feature of a laptop is always supported or fully operational. The main devices which may cause trouble are graphic chip, infrared (IrDA) port, soundcard, PCMCIA controller, plug-and-play devices and internal modem. Try to get as much information about these items as you can before buying a laptop. However, often it is very difficult to get the necessary information. Sometimes even the specifications or the helpline of the manufacturer aren't able to provide the information. Depending on your needs, you might investigate one of the vendors that provide laptops preloaded with Linux. By purchasing a preloaded Linux laptop, much of the guesswork and time spent downloading additional packages could be avoided.

I believe that Linux will come preinstalled on many more desktops and laptops in the not so distant future. But until that time, there will be some frustration with matching the appropriate hardware that Linux will support. Persevere and you will not be disappointed.

Linux for Mac and PowerPC platforms

Software options are opening up for Mac users who want to run PowerPC versions of the Linux operating system. There is much development in the Apple Mac and PowerPC world. SuSE Linux have just recently completed SuSE Linux 6.4 for the PowerPC platform. It will also use YaST2 for the installation, and the look and feel of the installed system will be identical to SuSE Linux on Intel systems minus the commercial applications because they are not available for Linux on PPC. In addition to PowerMacs, it will also run on other systems using the PowerPC processor, like the IBM RS/6000. Some more information about it can be found at **www.suse.com/ppc/** (Figure 5.24). There is a wealth of information at this site for anyone who wants to run his or her Mac on SuSE Linux.

There is much development in this area and there are many companies involved in this sector. Another very useful site is MkLinux, which did the first Mach micro kernel-based Linux distribution for the Apple Power Macintosh. It is estimated that there are somewhere between 50,000 and 100,000 MkLinux users. Check out **www.mklinux.org/** (Figure 5.25).

The main site for information, with an excellent mailing list archive, is **http://linuxppc.org/** (Figure 5.26). For hints and tips on how to use Linux on the Apple Power Macintosh check out **www.linuxppc.com/** (Figure 5.27).

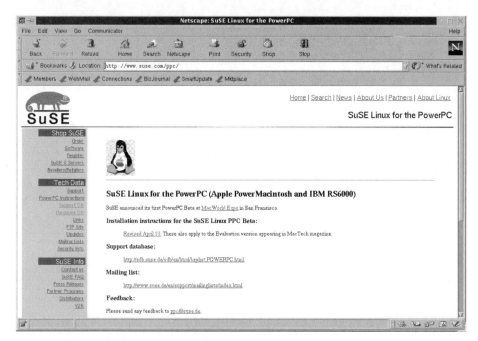

Figure 5.24   SuSE Linux for Macs and PowerPCs

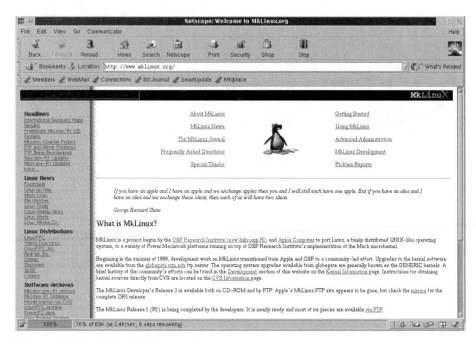

Figure 5.25   The MkLinux site

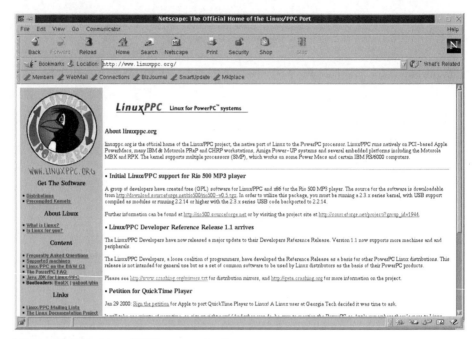

Figure 5.26   LinuxPPC support site

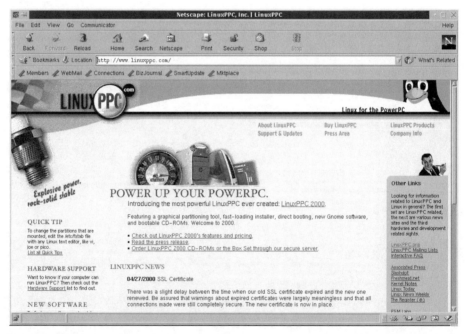

Figure 5.27   Linux on the PowerPC

Games

Linux is not a platform which is instantly associated with games. The public perception is of Linux as a command-line environment, but SuSE Linux has YaST2 – a properly installed set-up with a decent window manager, installed sound support and various media players, which is a reasonable multimedia platform.

Some people have already noticed this. In particular, Loki Entertainment Software has noticed this. Loki is a smallish startup from California, which has acquired the rights to port several successful PC games to the Linux platform. They can be found at **www.lokigames.com/** (Figure 5.28).

Figure 5.28 Loki Entertainment Software

Their first release is a port of *Civilization: Call to Power*, at **www.suse.de/uk/produkte/games/civ/index.html** (Figure 5.29).

SuSE Linux also offers the sequel to the legendary game *Railroad Tycoon*, *Railroad Tycoon II*, which puts gamers in control of 34 cargo types and 51 train engines from around the world: **www.suse.de/uk/produkte/games/rt2/index.html** (Figure 5.30).

Figure 5.29 Civilization: Call to Power game

Figure 5.30 The Railway Tycoon II game

The latest title in the best-selling Heretic-Hexen game series is a third-person action game, *Heretic II*, which sets players on a quest through vast city and outdoor environments where they search for a cure to a deadly evil plague before all is lost. It can be found at **www.suse.de/uk/produkte/games/ heretic_II/index.html** (Figure 5.31).

Figure 5.31   The Heretic II game

Eric's Ultimate Solitaire is much more than a deck of cards for your computer. It includes 23 of the most challenging and inventive solitaire games ever devised. You will be absorbed at **www.suse.de/uk/produkte/games/ solitaire/index.html** (Figure 5.32).

There are now many commercial games for Linux so, as they say at SuSE, have a lot of fun playing them!

Figure 5.32   23 versions of solitaire

Printing

Linux probably would not exist if it were not good at handling the tedious job of putting ink, or toner, on paper. When UNIX was first developed within AT&T's research labs, much of the work was funded internally on the promise of developing a low-cost document editing and typesetting system for the labs.

UNIX machines were first deployed within AT&T for document processing, in the early 1970s before the personal computer and the modern word processor existed.

When you install SuSE Linux you install a print server. You can plug a variety of printers into any Linux box and tell the lpr (line printer) subsystem about them; thereafter, you can rely on this system to maintain queues of pending print jobs for each printer and do various interesting things to them. If this sounds mundane, it is worth remembering that DOS had no such facility; while Windows and MacOS have print spoolers, UNIX had one nearly a decade before those operating systems were written and can still show them some effective tricks.

The most common print subsystem today is the Remote Printing ring, LPRng. It consists of a group of command-line tools and an lpd (line printer daemon), which listens for incoming print jobs and controls everything. You configure lpd by editing a file called `/etc/printcap`, although most Linux distributions use graphical tools to hide this from you (YaST in SuSE's case).

One feature of lpd is that you can tell it to send all incoming print files through a chain of filters (pieces of software that reformat the documents in various ways).

A universal trick, which all the major distributions play, is to try to turn all incoming print jobs into PostScript; then, if you do not have a PostScript-capable printer, to feed them to GhostScript. GhostScript is basically a PostScript language interpreter; it reads PostScript files in at one end and generates a graphical bitmap to send down the wire to your printer. Unless you have an unintelligent printer, for which there are no GhostScript drivers, or an ancient daisy-wheel printer, you will be able to configure your Linux system to use it as the output side of a colour PostScript printer.

Another handy thing is that the printer does not have to be connected to your current machine. You can print to a network printer, as long as it has an Internet address, or even to the lpd daemon on another UNIX or Linux system over the Internet, as long as it has permission to receive print jobs from your machine (granted in the `/etc/hosts.lpd` file) and recognises you as a known user. It is also possible (with a little work) to set up a print queue recognised by lpd that feeds documents into a fax server's queue, if you have suitable fax software installed on your system, such as mgetty.

Linux comes with a selection of tools for manipulating PostScript files. Some are part of the GhostScript package; ps2pdf, for example, takes PostScript files and turns them into Adobe Acrobat PDF files, suitable for transfer to other machines). The very practical mpage filter takes any old text file and turns it into a PostScript image with headers and footers and can print it two-up or four-up on the paper. On the Macintosh and PC interoperability side, both the Netatalk (Appletalk server) and Samba (SMB server) systems come with the ability to make a Linux print queue show up as a networked printer to Mac or Windows machines on the same network.

All of the above means that if you have a 486PC with, say, 8Mb of RAM and a 120Mb hard disk, along with a cheap laser printer and an Ethernet card, you can configure the 486 to print on the laser printer while making it look like a networked PostScript printer to the other machines on your local area network (LAN), all of which will save you a few hundred pounds if a networked PostScript laser printer is something you need.

I have used my trusty Kyocera printer on many Linux installations and never had a problem. Kyocera printers appeal to me for their reliability, economy and their eco-friendly features. Check them out at **www.printer.kyocera.de** (Figure 5.33).

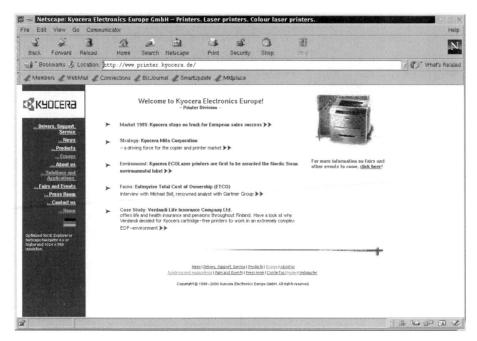

Figure 5.33   The Kyocera site

The Business Aspect of SuSE

In this chapter you will learn some background information on SuSE – the company, how it started, how it has evolved and where it is today – some of the many commercial implications of Linux and the main open source products.

SuSE

SuSE, pronounced zoo-zee, was established in Germany in 1992, making it one of the oldest Linux companies. The stamp of the company's four founders, three mathematicians and one computer scientist, all of whom hold masters degrees, is apparent in the meticulous development of its software and in SuSE's commitment to open source software development.

SuSE's goal is to manage the continuous changes in Linux by bundling and issuing its version changes with mission-critical applications firmly in mind and to provide world-class consulting and services to its business partners.

SuSE is the leading distribution of Linux in Europe has 12 offices in Germany, the UK, the USA, Italy, France and the Czech Republic, and over 50,000 installed business customers. The attendees of Linux World Expo in February 2000 voted SuSE Linux the Show Favorite Distribution, as they had the previous year.

SuSE Inc., SuSE's North American subsidiary, located in Oakland, California, provides consulting, technical support, Premier Partner programmes and sales support to customers, resellers and distributors.

SuSE Linux offers the most comprehensive packages of Linux-based applications. SuSE Linux is available both on CD-ROM and DVD, being the first Linux distribution to be so available. Version 6.4 featured over 1500 applications as well as a remarkably simple installation process. Targeted at both the desktop and the server market, this encyclopaedic library of tools also includes resources for software developers, Linux users, network administrators and businesses such as:

Did you know that...?

Base Linux

When you install Linux for the first time, the base Linux has to be brought up first. It works without the hard disk, which is not accessible at this point. Its kernel is on the boot disk or on CD-ROM. The root image (also on CD-ROM or on the boot disk) is loaded into a RAM disk. The other programs (for example, YaST) are also loaded into the RAM disk. After the first login, you start YaST and prepare for installing the 'real' Linux.

- the latest Linux kernel technology (2.2.14), with its impressive performance, networking and multimedia hardware support advances;

- customisable, user-friendly KDE and GNOME desktop environments;

- Informix SE, MySQL and PostgresSQL databases.

SuSE Holding AG, based in Nuremberg and the parent company for all other SuSE branches, is a privately owned company. Its four founders, Roland Dyroff, Thomas Fehr, Hubert Mantel and Burchard Steinbild, and a group of employees currently privately own SuSE.

The successful initial public offering (IPO) of Red Hat Software in August 1999 has brought the Linux operating system to the attention of investors in a way that could never have been imagined before. Red Hat, a Linux distributor, is now capitalised at £3.9 billion. Meanwhile, other companies in the Linux market have also gone public. Well-known examples are Caldera and VA Linux, the latter of which has enjoyed the attention of investors. SuSE is currently also working on their IPO, although no definitive date for this step has been confirmed yet. Being one of the rare examples in the Linux market that has already enjoyed healthy revenues in 1999, SuSE's IPO is likely to be a success.

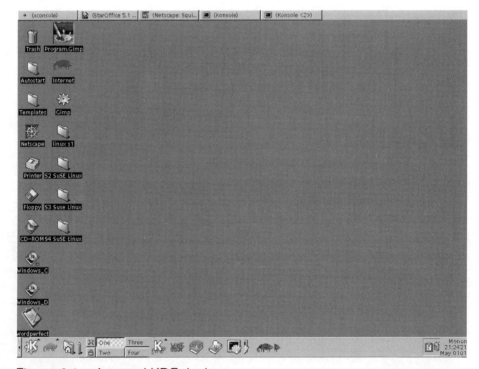

Figure 6.1   A typical KDE desktop

When you compare SuSE's revenues to those of Red Hat, it appears that SuSE is the largest Linux distributor in the world in terms of revenues, with sales of £15.2 million in 1999 versus some £10.3 million for Red Hat. Licence revenues are similar for the two at around £6.9 million.

International Data Corporation (IDC) statistics show Linux to be the fastest growing operating system in the market, with a current volume share of 25 per cent of the server market. Linux should continue to experience strong market share gains in the server market and the significant penetration of the desktop is promising in the medium term. Figure 6.1 shows a CDE desktop.

Open source versus closed source software

The code for any program can be presented basically in one of two formats: in machine-readable binaries (zeros and ones) or in human-readable source code. It is extremely difficult, indeed almost impossible, to alter any program if one only has access to the binaries and the program remains closed. Access to the human-readable source code allows a user to modify the program according to their needs.

Nearly all of the code of the packaged applications vendors such as Microsoft, SAP, Oracle and so on is closed source. These companies regard their source code as proprietary knowledge developed from their own investment in R&D and believe that releasing such code would be to lose a major competitive advantage.

Open source groups are developing software that in many cases challenges the closed source companies. Having supplied much of the software that provides the infrastructure of the Internet the open source movement is now making deep inroads into the operating systems market with Linux and is more and more aiming at the applications or end-user market.

Did you know that...?

Basic Input Output System (BIOS)

Every PC includes a small memory area containing the BIOS. This is a system of programs for executing basic operations connected to the hardware such as memory check and recognising hard drives. In Linux, the BIOS is not active, since it runs in real mode, and is switched off by the kernel at boot time. The Linux kernel has much more powerful capabilities than the BIOS.

It is comparatively easy to define the difference between open and closed source software. It is much more complex to determine what is truly open source software. Many different forms of licensing exist, which offer different strains of open source software, and there is much animosity over which of these licences can be truly labeled open source. The different types of licences are an important topic when looking at a distributor such as SuSE, as they affect the ability to commercialise the software and to attract developers to maintain and modify the code.

Microsoft's leaked internal review of the open source movement, nicknamed the Halloween documents, can be seen at **www.opensource.org/halloween/** (Figure 6.2).

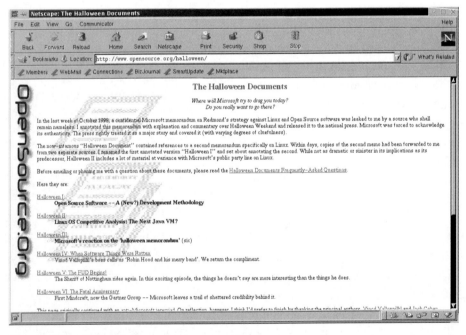

Figure 6.2 The 'Haloween documents'

Within these memos there was an overview of the types of software licensing available and those applicable to open source.

Though there are many types of software available free of charge, the open source stipulation is to have the source code available and modifiable. There are, however, variants on this, for example, Sun's Community Source License under which it releases the source code for Java, Jini and now Solaris. The licences are different principally in terms of the amount of control exerted over the code by the group which maintains it and the freedom that is given to others to make closed derivatives. Another example is the Mozilla License that is widely considered to be more business-friendly.

The type of licence applied to most components of a Linux distribution is called Copyleft, the principal form of which is the GNU Public License or GPL. This is critically different to all the others in that any modifications to the code must be kept open source. This means that it is not legally possible to add proprietary code and create a different/closed version of the software that could be sold commercially. Copyleft is also discussed earlier in this book.

The open source community divides broadly into two camps: those that believe that the GPL is the only proper and moral way to license open source software, such as the Free Software Foundation, and those that have a less restrictive outlook on licencing, as long as the code is freely modifiable, i.e. the Open Source Group. This last group distinguishes open source software as superior to closed software, because they believe that the development process will produce a superior product. They represent the more commercial arm of the open source movement and are keen to co-operate with big businesses in order to further the penetration of open source software. The former believe it is wrong to hoard software by having proprietary code and as such represent a less business-friendly strain of open source.

What are the implications of this to SuSE?

The SuSE distribution contains components with licences of all types. It also contains its own proprietary software, the set-up tool YaST. While FSF (Free Software Foundation) advocates might cringe at the assortment of licences in the SuSE distribution, that is not the case for the Open Source Group, to which Linus Torvalds belongs. Consequently there is an effective commercially oriented group of developers supporting what SuSE is doing.

What is the source of all the free software?

The Open Source Software movement began in universities in the USA in the early 1970s where it grew out of the UNIX community. The UNIX operating system was developed at AT&T's Bell Labs in 1969. However, since AT&T was a government-regulated monopoly, it was not allowed to compete in the computer business. As a result it licensed UNIX to universities for a nominal fee, and students could have access to the source code and alter it as they wished. The changes could then be shared between anyone with a licence. This built up into having an abundance of UNIX experts in the educational centres of the USA who learned to develop code together and to fix bugs as soon as they arose. These programmers went on to create the infrastructure for the Internet, the bulk of which is open source and freely downloadable. In turn the Internet enabled communication between widely dispersed developers, which became the development model for projects such as Linux.

Definition of free software

The following quote is from the FSF founder, Richard Stallmann:

The term 'free software' is sometimes misunderstood; it has nothing to do with price. It is about freedom. Here, therefore, is the definition of free software: a program is free software, for you, a particular user, if:

- *You have the freedom to run the program, for any purpose.*

- *You have the freedom to modify the program to suit your needs.*
  (To make this freedom effective in practice, you must have access to the source code, since making changes in a program without having the source code is exceedingly difficult.)

- *You have the freedom to redistribute copies, either gratis or for a fee.*

- *You have the freedom to distribute modified versions of the program, so that the community can benefit from your improvements.*

Since 'free' refers to freedom, not to price, there is no contradiction between selling copies and free software. In fact, the freedom to sell copies is crucial: collections of free software sold on CD-ROMs are important for the community, and selling them is an important way to raise funds for free software development. Therefore, a program which people are not free to include on these collections is not free software.

While Linux is the name under which most of us know the operating system distributed by companies such as SuSE and Red Hat, the FSF, in particular Richard Stallman, is responsible for the creation of a large number of the crucial operating system components that make up the whole system. Linux just relates to the system kernel. Many of the other components come from Richard Stallman's GNU Project, discussed below.

The GNU Project

Stallman wanted to create an operating system that was based on UNIX but offered an open source and freely downloadable alternative to the many commercial variants of UNIX available at the time (the project started in 1984). This was the starting point for the bottom-up rebuild of the UNIX operating system that has led to Linux. GNU components now make up a large part of any distributor's offering. Some of these components are as follows (see Figure 6.3):

- CC (GNU C Compiler) – the most widely used compiler in academia and the OS world.

- GNU Emacs originally a powerful character-mode text editor, over time Emacs was enhanced to provide a front end to compilers, mail readers, and so on.

- GNU GhostScript (PostScript printer/viewer) – this is a good example of how to combine commercial software and business; GhostScript is released in a commercial and a free version.

- GNOME GUI for Linux.

The GNU Project has created almost every component of a UNIX-like operating system, except the kernel. Despite the fact that there is a kernel in production, the GNU HURD, it is not yet ready for use. This has not made a difference: as Torvalds Linus created the Linux kernel in 1991, and since then, the blending of the Linux kernel and the GNU components have been known as the Linux Operating System.

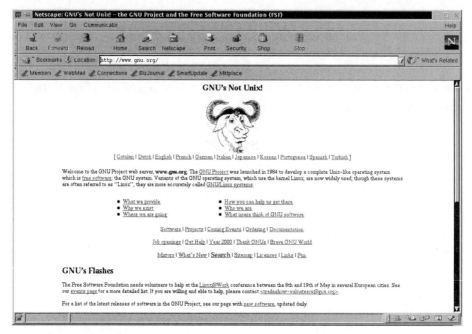

Figure 6.3 The GNU Project

The Open Source Group

The Open Source Group was founded in April 1998 when Netscape released the source code to Netscape Navigator to the public. It was a clear attempt by some open source advocates to distance themselves from the anti-commercial stance of the FSF. It was also to make the distinction that the software is not given away for nothing. They have liaised with the business community and tried to influence proprietary software developers such as SAP and Oracle to develop for the open source platforms, especially GNU/Linux. They aim to get rid of the notion that open source software is great for programmers but that real companies cannot rely upon it.

A key member of the open source movement is Eric Raymond, a prolific writer. His influential stance on why the open source software movement, with its thousands of unco-ordinated developers and constant releases, is superior to the monolithic planned commercial approach is called the Cathedral and the Bazaar, **www.tuxedo.org** (Figure 6.4). Raymond has also encouraged companies to make money from open source software.

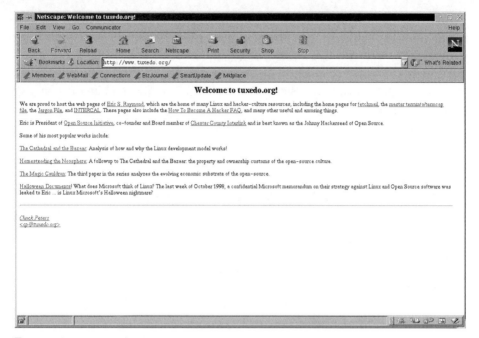

Figure 6.4 tuxedo.org

The Family of open source Internet software products

There are many successful open source products, several of which form the backbone of the Internet, for example Sendmail, BIND, Apache, PERL, Python, and Netscape. The high hopes for Linux rest not least upon the success of Apache, which has around a 55 per cent share of the Web server market, well above Microsoft's 22 per cent, and of Sendmail, the mail transport agent that has a 75 to 80 per cent market share.

The Linux Operating System

The development of Linux, as outlined in Raymond's the Web site, marks a revolution in the way software is developed. Before Linux, though open source software was commonly used, especially on the Internet, no one had developed software in the highly distributed way in which Linus Torvalds created the Linux kernel. The fact that an operating system kernel is a highly complex piece of coding makes it even more remarkable that it could be developed by a group of programmers over the Internet. On its own, the kernel was of limited use, but the reason for its success is that it was the missing link in the GNU Project's attempt to create an open source version of UNIX. Linus began to adapt the kernel to the GNU software such that there was a complete operating system. The system was copylefted and is now sold under the GNU GPL. The next section charts the history and development of SuSE Linux.

The SuSE Linux history

1991

Users: 1
Linus Torvalds, 21, hacks together makeshift operating system dubbed 'Linux'. After mentioning project on Internet software news- group, he posts program for downloading. Ten people download program, five send back bug fixes, code improvements and new features. By December more than 100 people worldwide join in Linux newsgroup and mailing lists.
Version: 0.01
Size: 10,000 lines of code

1992

Users: 1,000
Fully functional desktop Linux operating system runs on Intel x86 chips. Graphical user interface added. S.u.S.E. GmbH founded by Roland Dyroff, Thomas Fehr, Hubert Mantel and Burchard Steinbild.
Version: 0.96
Size: 40,000 lines of code

1993

Users: 20,000
More than 100 programmers contribute changes to code. Torvalds delegates code review duties to 'core' group of five. S.u.S.E. distributes Slackware on floppy disks and offers support for it; places ads in computer magazines. First sales of Linux system software:
Version: 0.99
Size: 100,000 lines of code

1994

Users: 100,000
Networking capability added. S.u.S.E. ships a Linux CD (SuSE Linux 1.0). Serving 4000 customers.
Version: Linux 1.0
Size: 170,000 lines of code

1995

Users: 500,000
Modified to run on Intel, Digital and Sun SPARC processors. Linux Journal circulation: 10,000. S.u.S.E. ships Linux with the installation tool (YaST) in April. Florian LaRoche joins the team and S.u.S.E. starts the development of its own Linux distribution.
Version: Linux 1.2
Size: 250,000 lines of code

1996

Users: 1,500,000
Can harness the computing power of several processors at once. SuSE Linux 4.2 is released
Version: Linux 2.0
Size: 400,000 lines of code

1997

Users: 3,500,000
Monthly Linux magazines started in Japan, Poland, Germany, Yugoslavia and the UK. New Linux version posted every week. S.u.S.E. opens offices in California as SuSE Inc.
Version: Linux 2.1
Size: 800,000 lines of code

1998

Users: 7,500,000
About 10,000 programmers involved in newsgroups, testing, code improvements. S.u.S.E. Linux 5.1 sells 40,000 units in four months from November 1997 to February 1998. Company name changes from S.u.S.E. to SuSE.
Version: Linux 2.1.110 (110th update of 2.1)
Size: 1.5 million lines of code

1999

Users: 14,000,000 to 18,000,000

First successful Linux IPO (Red Hat), first International Data Group (IDG) shows about Linux with huge response both from exhibitors and visitors (the show floor doubled between the two shows in March and August. In May, SuSE releases SuSE Linux 6.1 and introduces Worldwide Business Partner Programs. SuSE Linux has received five 'Best Linux Distribution' awards to date in 1999. SuSE Inc. moves to larger offices to accommodate growth. In June there are 50,000 business customers worldwide. Q1 growth is 230 over Q1 from previous year. SuSE releases financial information to press. July: SuSE adds the Alpha platform to its product offerings by releasing SuSE Linux 6.1 for Alpha AXP. August: SuSE releases SuSE Linux 6.2. November: Intel and Apax fund SuSE. December: Dirk H. Hohndel becomes chief technical officer of SuSE AG. SuSE Linux 6.3 is released on CD-ROM and DVD with 1500 applications.

Version: Linux 2.3.23 (as of 27 November 1999)

Size: 2.1 million lines of code

2000

April: SuSE Linux 6.4 is released on CD-ROM and DVD with a new installation. PPC and Alpha versions of SuSE Linux 6.4 to follow shortly.

What are the quality controls in Linux?

Because all programmers are free to work on the Linux kernel and to contribute their ideas, there is still substantial control over the whole process monitored by Linus Torvalds, who generally has the last word on any debatable issues. He delegates a lot of the day-to-day scrutiny to a handful of trusted colleagues. The continual beta processing indicates that many ideas compete for a place within the kernel and there is consequently a great deal of effort involved, thus leading to extremely high-quality code. This is different to the situation in a commercial organisation where an individual may be assigned to a project for which he is not best suited or where an individual may consider a project complete while others might disagree. Additionally the response time of the Linux community is faster than any commercial organisation. If, for example, there is a virus attack, there will typically be a patch posted to the Internet within hours, compared to days or weeks for the larger commercial vendors.

The vast number of developers working on Linux and their constant posting of patches and improvements to the Internet mean that it has caught up rapidly with other versions of UNIX, and is now considered by many to be far more stable than these versions. Many believe the same is true of Linux versus NT, a claim that the market statistics are progressively supporting.

The position of Linux within the OS market

Because Linux can be freely downloaded over the Internet and freely copied, the information on the actual number of users is difficult to obtain. On some counts there are an estimated 14 million users of Linux at present (see **www.counter.li.org**).

IDC only tracks the paid copies of Linux in distribution, which is in fact more pertinent to SuSE. In 1998 the worldwide server operating system market was, according to IDC, worth some £3.45 billion. The client operating system environment was worth slightly more at £4.1 billion.

According to IDC, the global revenues from Linux in 1998 were an estimated £59 million, with £38 million of that coming from the client side. The server revenues are by far the fastest growing, experiencing nearly 140 per cent revenue growth in 1998 versus 1997. In terms of revenues, the low price of the Linux operating system means that Linux has a very small but rapidly rising share of the overall market.

Though Linux has less than one per cent share of the market by measurable revenues, the picture is quite different if we look at volume shipments. According to IDC, Linux had a 25 per cent (from latest IDC reports for 1999, February 2000) market share of the worldwide server operating environment market in 1998, having experienced 180 per cent growth in 1998 versus 1997.

Looking at the IDC figures there is clearly the potential for an increase in the size of the worldwide Linux market in the coming years. This of course will be matched by a similar increase in the market for Linux services, benefiting the Linux distributors.

Why Linux poses a threat to established operating systems

The principal benefit that Linux has over the existing closed source operating systems is the number of developers working on it from all over the world. This has been an important motivational strength in the creation of open source software. To a great extent it has been done simply because developers had a problem that they needed to solve and did so.

The Linux operating system is a serious challenger to much older systems in terms of stability, scalability and functionality. The last major upgrade to the Linux kernel (version 2.2) was in January 1999. There is on average one developer release per week and more stable releases about once a month.

The aspiration of being the world's dominant operating system is now clearly in the sights of the developers and, if anything, this is likely to stimulate development even more. Linux distributors will now pay programmers to develop the system that is their principal source of revenue. The development of Linux is one of very speedy conversion to any of the characteristics of existing operating systems and it is catching up steadily.

Linux comes at a much lower cost than traditional operating systems. It is not, as many people believe, free. As discussed earlier, to have a stable version of a software program a company needs a distributor who can provide updates and patches, and there are considerable service and support costs associated with using Linux, as there are with any other operating system. To give an example of costs, you can buy Windows NT workstation online for under £200. You can buy SuSE online for abut £35.

What can you run on Linux?

Linux has been a success in the server environment. This has been due to the fact that it has offered a cheap, non-resource hogging platform that is readily compatible with a variety of open source applications. The availability of applications is a key factor for any operating system. On top of the open source contributions there is an ever-increasing number of commercial applications that have been ported to Linux, such as Oracle and SAP.

Linux is available on the desktop and has been found to be stable and reliable. It can be used to surf the Web, send and receive emails, do word-processing, and so on.

One of the greatest barriers to running Linux in either the home or workstation environment is the difficulty of installation. This is true of any operating system, and the difficulties of installing Linux are no greater than those of installing any system. I can now install SuSE Linux in 25 minutes whereas it takes me well over an hour to install Windows. The SuSE distribution is praised for its easy-to-use installation tool, YaST2, and this is improving all the time. This debate of installation problems should cease as vendors offer preinstalled systems.

Preinstalled Linux systems have now been offered not only by Linux specialists, but also by leading players such as Dell, Compaq, HP and IBM. Having Linux on your PC does not prevent you from running Windows applications. If you have the hard drive space you can install both and run either.

There is an enormous amount of quality applications software available that runs on Linux. Applix and Star Division both offer integrated suites of powerful desktop programs – word processors (see Figure 6.5), spreadsheets, graphics applications and so on. Corel offers a version of CorelDraw in addition to the existing Linux port of WordPerfect. There is an Adobe Photoshop replica (GIMP), games and a variety of other applications.

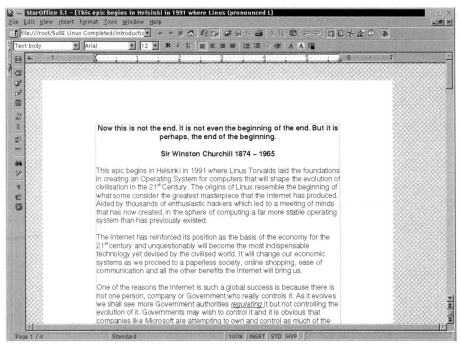

Figure 6.5 A StarOffice screenshot of the introduction of this book

Netscape Mozilla project

The source code to Netscape's Navigator browser is managed by an entity known as Mozilla. The licence is not pure GPL as Netscape reserves the final right to reject/force modifications into the Mozilla codebase and Netscape's engineers are the appointed area directors of large components. The browser is, however, an essential addition to any of the Linux distributions. Visit **www.mozilla.org/** (Figure 6.6) for details.

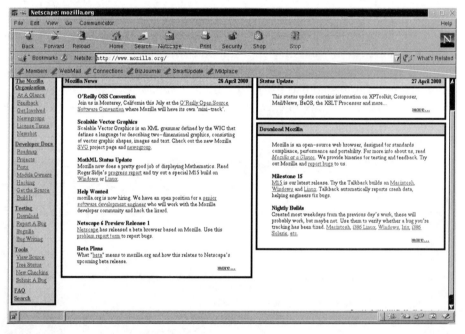

Figure 6.6 Netscape Mozilla project

Apache

The Apache Web server is one of the highest-profile, most successful of the open source projects. In 1995 the most popular server software on the Web was the public domain HTTP daemon developed by the National Center for Supercomputing Applications, University of Illinois, Urbana-Champaign. However, development of this stalled during 1994, and many Web masters had developed their own extensions and bug fixes that were in need of a common distribution. A small group of these Web masters, connected via email, gathered together for the purpose of co-ordinating their changes in the form of patches. By February 1995, eight core contributors formed the foundation of the original Apache group. Less than a year after the group was formed, the Apache server was the number one server on the Internet.

Netcraft's survey of Web servers shows how this particular open source product has gained a market share of over 50 per cent and has more than held its own against Microsoft's Internet information server.

Perl

Originally developed in 1986 by Larry Wall, Perl (Practical Extraction and Report Language) has become the language of choice for system and network administration as well as for CGI programming. It is the standard scripting language for all Apache Web servers. Perl has the ability to hold together many different processes. Large sites such as Netscape, Yahoo, CNET, Amazon and Excite make extensive use of Perl in managing their sites and providing interactive services. Perl is now maintained by a core group of about 100 programmers who keep in contact via the perl5porters mailing list. Larry Wall retains artistic control over the language itself, but a well-defined extension mechanism has led to the development of over 600 add-on modules developed by independent programmers. See **www.perl.org/** (Figure 6.7) for details.

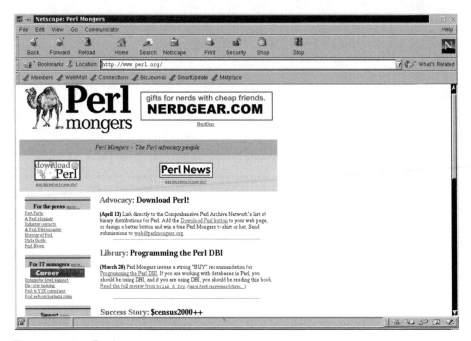

Figure 6.7   Perl

Sendmail

Originally developed by Eric Allman in 1981, Sendmail (**www.sendmail.org/**) is the dominant mail transport agent on the Internet, with an estimated 75 to 80 per cent market share.

Regardless of the email program used to create email, any mail that goes beyond the local site is generally routed via a mail transport agent. Given the number of 'hops' any given Internet mail message takes to reach its destination, it is likely that virtually every piece of Internet email is handled by a Sendmail server somewhere along the route. Sendmail is used by most Internet service providers and shipped as the standard MTA solution by all major UNIX vendors, including Sun, HP, IBM, Compaq and SGI.

Did you know that...?

Account

This is a combination of login and password. In general, the system administrator creates the user account. He also assigns one or more groups to the user, as well as the resulting permissions. Creating a user account normally includes assigning a home directory and the delivery of email.

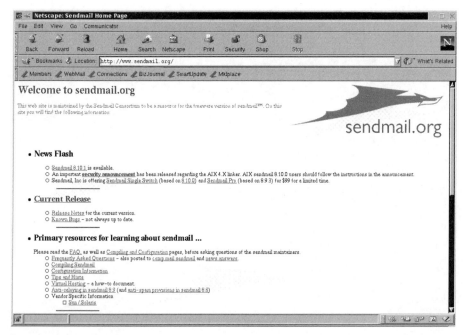

Figure 6.8   Sendmail

Eric Allman has since set up a company that will deliver a commercial version of Sendmail. The company will continue to enhance and release the freeware product with source code and the right to modify and redistribute. The new commercial product line will focus on cost effectiveness with Web-based administration (Figure 6.8).

BIND

BIND (Berkeley Internet Name Domain) **(www.isc.org/)** is not well known outside the technical elite, but IT professionals are familiar with the service BIND makes possible: the domain naming system (DNS). The network of BIND servers that make up the DNS translates native Internet addresses such as 254.28.58.201 into the form everyone has come to know: names such as **ibm.com, amazon.com** or **eworldhandbook.com**. Originally developed in 1984 by Paul Mockapetris, the DNS is currently maintained by Paul Vixie under the auspices of the Internet Software Consortium (ISC), an organisation formed by Rick Adams when he switched Uunet's status from non-profit to commercial in 1993 (Figure 6.9).

The DNS, along with the rest of the Berkeley TCP/IP suite, forms the foundation for the entire Internet industry, including ISPs, content providers, and value-added software companies.

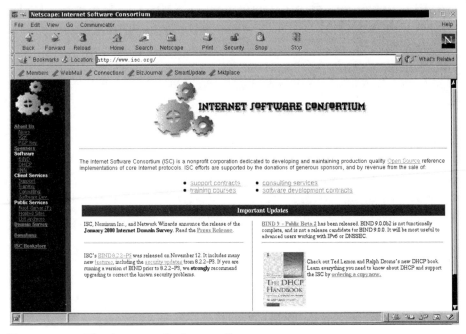

Figure 6.9   The Internet Software Consortium site

Gimp

Gimp is an acronym for GNU Image Manipulation Program. It is a freely distributed piece of software suitable for such tasks as photo retouching, image composition and image authoring. It is effectively an Adobe Photoshop clone for UNIX/Linux workstations.

WINE

WINE (Wine is not an emulator) is an OS windows emulation library for UNIX. WINE competes (somewhat) with Sun's discontinued WABI project, which is non-OS. To ease the migration to other PC compatibility products on Sun, WABI 2.2 will continue to be supported and available from Sun as an unbundled product. WINE is the crucial piece of software that allows Windows applications such as Microsoft Office to be run on Linux. While still a developer's release, there are numerous examples of older versions of MS Office running on Linux using WINE. There are rumours that it is even possible to run Lotus Notes clients under Linux with WINE.

SAMBA

SAMBA (**www/samba.org/**) provides an SMB file server for UNIX. Recently, the SAMBA team has managed to reverse engineer and develop an NT domain controller for UNIX as well. For most networks, SAMBA's role can be summarised by saying that Samba provides a complete replacement for Windows NT, Warp, NFS or Netware servers. The SAMBA home page can be seen in Figure 6.10.

Squid

Squid is a high-performance proxy-caching server (**www.squid-cache.org/**) for Web clients, supporting FTP, gopher and HTTP data objects. It is popular with large international ISPs (see Figure 6.11).

KDE and GNOME

These are the open source GUIs that provide a user interface resembling the popular Windows or Mac GUIs.

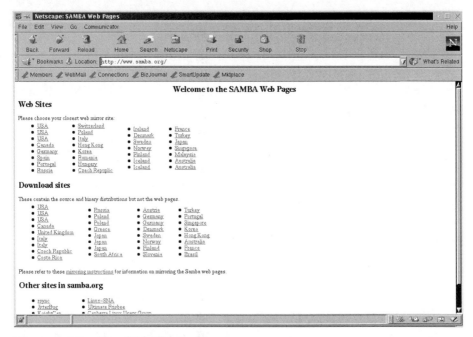

Figure 6.10   The SAMBA home page

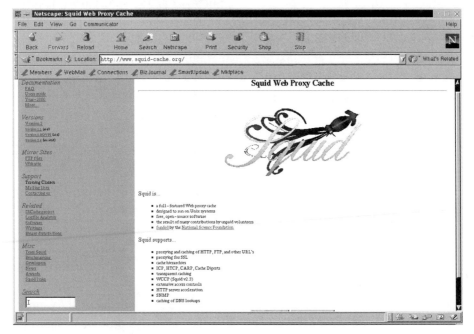

Figure 6.11   Squid Web Proxy Cache

Power to the people

The latest bulletin from 'Linux Power' suggests Linux is starting to appear on more and more corporate servers, running alongside or even replacing Netware and Windows NT. That's an advanced state of affairs for 'free' software. This revolution is taking place because Linux is more reliable than Windows, the source code is open, and the cost of ownership is lower. Microsoft and Novell may not be running scared as yet, but they know this is a real threat to their earnings source. According to internal Microsoft memos recently leaked to the press, 'Linux poses a significant near-term revenue threat to Windows NT.'

One part of the IT community views Linux as a viable choice, but another segment does not as yet. Microsoft is quick to point out the shortcomings in Linux and is eager to brand Linux as a low-end system with niche appeal. Microsoft says the Linux hype has caused people to take its claims of reliability at face value. It is ironic that the world's largest software company feels threatened, given the Linux market's fragmentation and the fact that Microsoft has always marketed the advantages of a single version of Windows.

Microsoft's attitude toward Linux was initially one of astonishment that corporate customers were willing to trust and invest in an operating system that did not have an identifiable company backing it, followed closely by a sense of frustration that many companies were adopting Linux. The bad feelings run in both directions. 'Microsoft isn't the disease, but they're a symptom,' says Eric Raymond. 'If your critical business processes are controlled by software whose insides you can't even see, that means you're on the wrong end of a monopoly. Prices will rise, and you'll pay more to be locked in.'

Many companies are now realising that the Linux development model creates higher-quality code and the beauty of Linux is in its simplicity.

Many people are currently facing the choice between tuning in, turning on, and installing Linux servers, or running them alongside commercial platforms. Making this decision means undertaking some operating system insight appraisal. Start with the big-picture issues: price, support, training and reliability. Then compare the competitors side by side to see how they stand up in a business environment. Can the underlying OS kernel scale to thousands of end users? Is the network directory up to the task of tracking resources and individuals? Does the operating system support the requisite protocols, and how efficient is its underlying file system? What about scripting tools for stress-free management?

Trying to manually update any operating system is a considerable task, but there is no need to feel alone. The Linux community provides a multitude of Web sites and bulletin boards bursting with freeware, shareware, testimonials, advice, tips, bug fixes, and endless discussions of the finer points of Linux. These resources typically replace the traditional technical support centres offered by proprietary software companies.

Magical mystery tour

This section looks at all the companies and organisations which are now working and collaborating with Linux.

The Linux operating system is a study of contradictions. It is free, but businesses are willing to pay for it. It is feature-rich, but lacks some functionality IT departments expect. It is reliable but not everyone in mission-critical projects are using it.

Linux is no longer a curiosity in business IT environments. According to a new survey by *InformationWeek* Research, 26 per cent of IT managers say their companies now use the operating system, up sharply from 14 per cent in March 1999 and up even more from the three per cent in 1998. Another 11 per cent of the 300 IT managers surveyed plan to deploy Linux within the next year. That means more than a third of businesses use or plan to use Linux. Not long ago, businesses were being asked, 'What's your Internet strategy?' Now they are being asked, 'What's your Linux strategy?'

That is a considerable accomplishment for a freeware operating system that was mainly popular with college students and Internet developers just a few years ago. What has changed? Linux has got its act together. Speciality providers such as SuSE and the other major distributions now offer Linux software packages with integrated tools, removing many of the do-it-yourself headaches of a downloaded operating system, while major technology vendors sell Linux on mainstream hardware platforms or are porting applications to it. Commercial service and support is also more readily available.

Cost is another important issue. Though Linux is available at no cost for downloading from the Internet, IT departments are willing to pay £35 for Linux CDs, which can then be loaded on to multiple machines. Compare that with Windows NT, which costs £100 per workstation upgrade and £1310 per server with 10 client licences. The savings from using Linux can add up quickly.

Among companies planning to deploy Linux within the next year, 72 per cent say they will use it to run a Web or intranet server. That said, Linux is increasingly being adopted for other kinds of applications. Oracle reports 100,000 downloads of the Linux version of its Oracle8i database by developers, which Oracle interprets as a sign of things to come. Linux is cheap, simple, and doesn't overly burden the user with a lot of administrative overhead; if one server breaks, you throw another in. It is almost a disposable operating system

IBM recently unveiled a reorganisation and product development strategy aimed at marketing Linux as a platform for companies engaged in e-business. IBM has created a Linux unit within its enterprise server group to ensure Linux runs smoothly on all its server platforms, port its enterprise software to the open-source operating system, and create an IBM-branded version of Linux suited for e-business requirements. See **www-4.ibm.com/software/is/mp/linux/** (Figure 6.12).

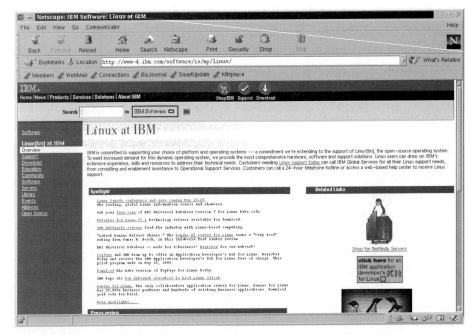

Figure 6.12   Linux and IBM

Compaq's Linux Alpha Server site asks the question, 'Why Alpha for Linux?' Compaq's answer is, 'Because our customers are doing amazing things with it.' Check it out at **www.digital.com/alphaserver/linux/alpha_linux.html** (Figure 6.13).

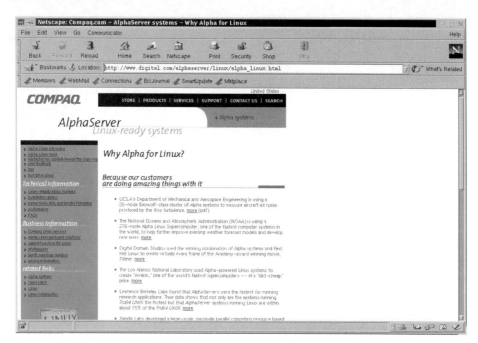

Figure 6.13   Linux and Compaq

At HP the support for Linux is staggering. Check it out at **www.internetsolutions. enterprise.hp.com/linux/** (Figure 6.14).

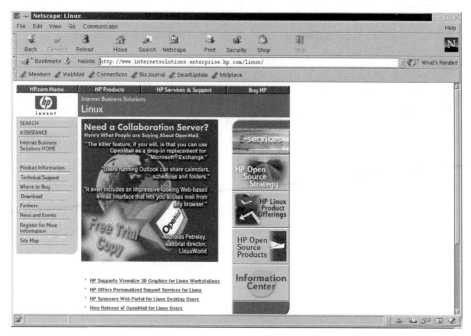

Figure 6.14   Linux and Hewlett-Packard

Console

Previously this was synonymous with terminal. In Linux, you have virtual consoles. This enables you to use one screen for many independently running sessions. In the standard runlevel 2, you have six virtual consoles which can be reached by pressing `Alt+F1` to `Alt+F6`. From within a running X Window System, you reach the text consoles by pressing `Ctrl+Alt+F1` to `Ctrl+Alt+F6`.

Dell is one of the first hardware manufacturers to preinstall Linux, thus eliminating many of the problems associated with installation, unsupported peripherals and missing drivers. I believe it will not be long before every hardware manufacturer is doing the same. Dell's Web site is **www.dell.com/us/en/biz/topics/ linux_linuxhome.htm** (Figure 6.15).

Sun supports Linux in many positive ways and you can download StarOffice from their Web site: **www.sun.com/software/linux/ position.html** (Figure 6.16).

SGI recently signed a deal with SuSE Linux for a joint engineering project to bring IRIS FailSafe, SGI's high-availability clustering software, to the Linux operating system. IRIS FailSafe running on Linux will enable a user to link two or more servers together so that one picks up the computing load should the other fail, allowing applications to increase availability to the level required for mission-critical data centre operations. This capability is an important component of the development of Linux in a business-computing environment. SGI's Linux Web site is at **www.sgi.com/linux/** (Figure 6.17).

Figure 6.15   Linux and Dell

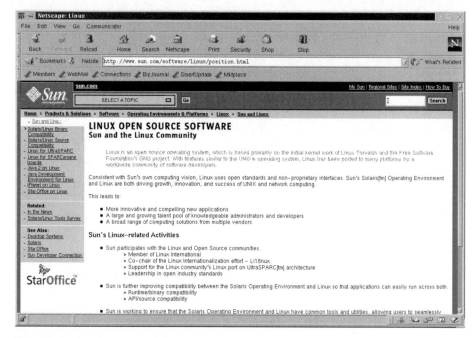

Figure 6.16   Linux and Sun

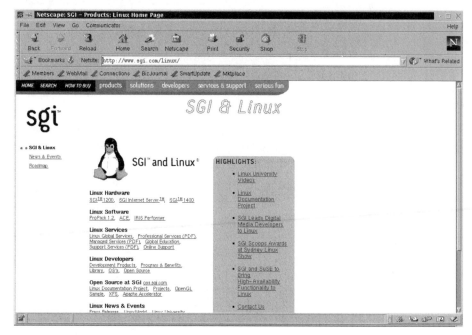

Figure 6.17   Linux and SGI

This kind of commitment is leading more IT managers to adopt Linux, which has historically crept into companies from the bottom up. According to the *InformationWeek* research survey mentioned earlier 86 per cent of all IT managers (and 92 per cent at companies with more than £345 million in annual revenue) say the support of large technology suppliers has made their companies more likely to deploy Linux.

In some ways, however, Linux is still in its infancy as an enterprise platform. Two-thirds of companies using Linux have been doing so for one year or less. And while Linux deployments are widening, they are not deep. Respondents to *InformationWeek's* survey say just four per cent of their total operating system environments consist of Linux. Two years from now, that figure is expected to rise to 15 per cent, which is impressive, but still far short of Windows' position.

Linux's main selling point is perhaps unsurprisingly its price, with 61 per cent of survey respondents citing low cost as a primary reason for using Linux. But that is closely followed by performance and reliability.

Linux is especially attractive to UNIX users who want to add commodity servers to an existing environment that they can manage without learning new skills. Linux servers don't crash or need rebooting for six months or a year at a time. Linux's popularity is fundamentally about the technology market's desire for choice. For a long time in the 1990s, it looked like the computer world was rapidly moving towards one in which consumers and corporate customers had no choice about the systems they ran, and that frightened a lot of people. Businesses were undecided about Microsoft, and even its supporters were reluctant to give control to any one company. Many people threw up their hands and said Microsoft would dominate with the versions of its operating system, and it would marginalise UNIX. No one could really see anything changing that situation. Then, in mid- to late 1998, database vendors began porting their software to Linux, and major systems vendors threw support behind Linux as well. Suddenly, this was a real effort with committed companies behind it.

Wall Street is now betting on a Linux boom. The operating system that grew up on the Internet, powering the Web page, application and caching servers that underpin the network, is suddenly reaping Internet-like valuations for the companies that distribute, preload and support it. As companies expose more of their back-end data through the Web, lines between infrastructure and back-office applications are blurred, pushing Linux more firmly into the arena of business-critical processing.

Will Linux fever last among investors? Open source supporters say Linux companies' valuations recognise that their unconventional development model is more effective than proprietary methods of development. The capital markets say this is a fundamentally better way of developing technology. But the cash pouring into Linux companies from high-tech vendors, venture capitalists and Wall Street investors is raising some questions. How do Linux companies build sustainable businesses selling software that is not tied to a traditional licence agreement? Can these suppliers make the software run well enough and provide the necessary development tools to make Linux a compelling alternative for running back-end e-business systems, thereby expanding the market? And, perhaps more importantly, can Linux satisfy enterprise customers' demands for a formal sales and support chain?

IT managers refer to the lack of business applications as among Linux's most-significant weaknesses, with two-thirds of survey respondents noting that complaint. Many software companies have not ported their software to Linux, as they feel there is not yet sufficient demand. This is changing daily as more software companies are realising they can lose market share quickly in this rapidly developing marketplace. For these reasons and others, Linux is not being adopted by all businesses. Technology suppliers are working to improve Linux's shortcomings as a platform for e-business, and more applications continue to become available. Oracle plans to ship its front-office suite, Oracle11i, on Linux. Oracle claims it only has 800 paying customers for the Linux edition of its database, accounting for about £4.1 million in revenue, compared with about £620 million for Windows NT products. Yet, Oracle is aware there was a time when NT too was only a £4.1 million business. IBM has ported its DB2, Domino, MQSeries, and WebSphere middleware to the platform, and its VisualAge for Java builder is available on Linux.

SuSE Linux is continually investing in three areas: technology that enhances its platform, online content for developers, and services and support. The clear trend among Linux suppliers is to expand their portfolios of related products and services. Because of the way the market is structured, the way to make money on Linux is to add more layers of value above the operating system. That is what vendors are hoping. Indeed, if there is one thing on which IT managers and Linux suppliers agree, it is the need for at least a few strong suppliers to emerge. They will see growth in their market share come directly from how they can differentiate themselves.

IBM has placed its Linux efforts under the control of its top enterprise systems executives to ensure that the operating system runs smoothly on the IBM hardware. IBM unveiled a reorganisation that places responsibility for its Linux strategy under senior VP Sam Palmisano, who reports directly to CEO Lou Gerstner. In a memo sent to Gerstner on 7 January 2000, Palmisano wrote that Linux will 'play a pivotal role' in meeting customers' demand for interoperable systems and heralds 'another important shift in the technology world'.

IBM has created a unit within its enterprise systems group to oversee all UNIX and Linux efforts. IBM dissolved the Internet division, saying a separate group was no longer necessary as e-business permeates every corner of the company's operations. As Linux matures, IBM watchers wonder how the company will handle the platform alongside AIX, the IBM UNIX variant that runs on its PowerPC RS/6000 servers, and Project Monterey, a version of UNIX for the PowerPC and Intel's upcoming 64-bit CPUs that combine elements of AIX, SCO, and Sequent's Dynix. Linux is the next-generation platform for e-business, and IBM is repositioning itself to take advantage of that. Linux seems to fit squarely in IBM's portfolio. To advance Linux's appeal to large companies, IBM plans to step up efforts to run Linux on its four core platforms – System/390, RS/6000, AS/400, and Netfinity middleware that enables interoperability between Linux servers and legacy systems, and develop scalability, availability and other enhancements to the Linux kernel that IBM could license to other suppliers.

Suppliers are also stepping up their efforts to broaden acceptance of the Linux operating system with a flurry of new products, support offerings and business partnerships. In the past Linux was seen as a niche operating system with a cult following but it is now gaining popularity among administrators of Web and departmental servers because of its stability and low cost of ownership.

However, Linux still has some hurdles to clear; it does not scale well beyond four processors, and installation can be difficult for non-technical users. Linux distributions are increasing their service and support to address those issues.

While Linux is emerging as a viable operating system at the server level, its suitability for business desktops is still a matter of debate. Critics contend that despite gains in ease of use, Linux still carries its 'techie' heritage, and the number of applications for the operating system place it in a niche-player status in the desktop world. But devotees counter that Linux is already much easier to install, maintain and use than it was just a year ago, and that software companies are beginning to unveil products ranging from vertical applications to integrated office suites to meet customer demand.

Critics of Linux come in all shapes and sizes, but supporters seem to be a remarkably consistent group. Companies that have embraced Linux are typically either those that have been UNIX users for some time or those that employ IT staff who champion the operating system. Everyday I hear of companies whose initial idea to use Linux originally came from a young graduate in the company's IT department. It is the recently graduated, who realise the power and potential of Linux from working with it at college and university, who are the real driving force in the adoption of Linux in today's business environments.

Linux's ability to satisfy companies' technical requirements is enhanced by the fact that it can do so very cheaply. Linux can be downloaded from the Internet for free or purchased from SuSE or any of the other distributions at a very low cost with a suite of utilities and other support software, services and documentation included. Add to that the fact that Linux runs efficiently even on 486 PCs, and companies looking to save money suddenly pay attention.

The cost of moving from one version of Windows to the next is enormous, and many companies are now choosing to move instead from Windows to a Linux-based suite of applications. It is not likely that the average knowledge worker will soon see his or her Microsoft Office applications swept aside in favour of a suite of Linux productivity software: ease of use, data compatibility between Linux and Windows systems and a larger variety of software will all have to have a little work done on them.

That said, there is some momentum in the software world, even in the office suites arena, a critical battleground in proving mainstream legitimacy. Corel has sold a Linux version of WordPerfect for some time, and Applix offers its ApplixWare integrated office suite for Linux. Sun Microsystems attracted a lot of attention with its acquisition of Star Division and its StarOffice suite for Linux, Windows, Solaris, and OS/2, which it will continue to make available for free. Like Linux itself, the package can be downloaded via the Internet, and Sun will make the source code for Star Portal, the Web-ready version of the product, available to suppliers and service providers who wish to host the product. If StarOffice addresses users' basic needs for tasks such as word processing and spreadsheeting, then a big roadblock to Linux on the desktop, the availability of general desktop applications, will be overcome. But also keep your eye on the KDE KOffice developments.

Linux application vendors acknowledge that there is often a gap between technical users' perceptions and end users' requirements. On the one hand, you have IT employees and senior management who want to save money and run things efficiently. On the other hand, you have users who are used to Microsoft Office and Windows in general, and who probably do not want change.

That raises the image of IT managers attempting to provide a solution to something few end users regard as a problem. The people most likely to adopt Linux on the desktop are those with a dislike of Microsoft from a business standpoint. Windows is adequate, and for most companies, that will remain good enough until the finance department realise the cost-saving benefits of Linux, and then things will change rapidly.

IBM recently unveiled a low-cost Netfinity server optimised for the Linux operating system. IBM also support and service the SuSE distribution as well as the other major Linux distributions. The IBM Netfinity 3500 M10 will include a driver that lets the open source operating system take advantage of RAID storage. Users can opt, through resellers or custom configuration, for preinstalled versions of SuSE, and use IBM as a single point of contact for hardware and software support. IBM is also launching a plan to work with independent software vendors to certify enterprise applications, such as SAP, for Linux on IBM hardware. Initially, it will work with SAP to certify its R/3 enterprise resource planning software. Although most major hardware vendors have more or less embraced Linux as the connective tissue for performing low-end file, print and Web serving, the challenge will be for other suppliers to compete on the level of professional services, where IBM has a clear competitive advantage.

When it comes to Linux support, IBM is putting its money where its mouth is as we have seen above. The company launched a global support program that is on par with that of its UNIX and Windows NT service offerings, in response to customer demand.

Among other things, IBM is offering those who purchase its Netfinity servers preloaded with different versions of Linux free service and support for 90 days. Direct telephone and email support will be offered around the clock in more than 164 countries for Netfinity servers. While this free offer may appear trivial, many customers said it is during those first 90 days when most problems occur. Furthermore, there are far fewer Linux specialists in IT organisations than there are Windows NT or UNIX professionals. The IBM Netfinity Web site is at **www.pc.ibm.com/ww/netfinity/linux/** (Figure 6.18)

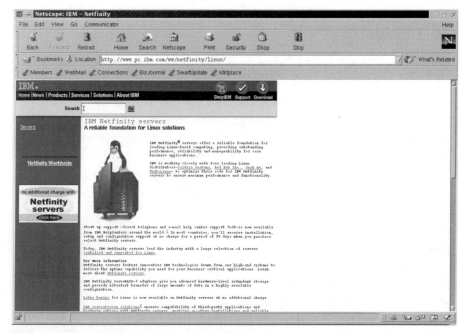

Figure 6.18   IBM Netfinity and LINUX

IBM is also expanding its education curriculum for Linux users, including both classroom and Web-based courses available through IBM Global Services. IBM also said its Linux-based servers will link to AS/400 servers with the release of Yellow Dog Linux Champion Server 1.1 from Terra Soft Solutions Inc.

Network architects who want a taste of the free life should know that open source servers can be deployed alongside Netware or NT machines or both. A free software utility known as Samba, available on many open source sites, allows Linux to deal with Microsoft Server Message Block (SMB) the protocol that NT, Windows 95 and Windows 98 machines use to exchange data. Once Samba is installed, Linux and BSD boxes are recognised as peers by Microsoft platforms.

It is the same story with Netware, except in this case the free utility is called Mars. The software emulates Netware 3.x, enabling open source servers to access file and print resources. Samba is an outstanding piece of freeware.

Software giants

Anything that worries Microsoft, and Linux certainly has, invariably interests other software companies. Many in the software industry have suddenly declared their support for open source software, with Microsoft apparently alone in its distrust of Linux. While most of these companies do not plan to change their business models radically by releasing their own proprietary source code to the public, they do recognise the advantages of aligning themselves with the open source movement. In return for their support, these companies cultivate a new user group and gain the support and input of an active community of developers.

Large software vendors are expressing their support in a number of ways. Netscape, by giving away its browser and releasing its source code, represents one extreme. IBM took another tack by deciding to bundle the open-source Apache server software with its WebSphere Internet commerce package; IBM is also offering free downloads of other early-stage software in exchange for developers' comments and suggestions. But by far the most common approach, taken by Hewlett-Packard, Oracle, Sun Microsystems, Informix and Computer Associates, has been to announce plans to port proprietary software to run on Linux.

This decision is primarily a response to a growing number of Linux users who are demanding vendor support for the operating system. The user community has brought Linux to their attention. It is not prohibitively expensive for software suppliers to port their products to Linux, although standard costs include hiring a team of engineers, providing customer support, working out bugs and making sure the partner channels are in place. In exchange for paying that price, though, software vendors gain the loyalty of a user base of roughly seven million programmers. Additionally, as Linux gains momentum, software vendors are afraid to appear imprudent by not embracing it. Linux is becoming a more controlled environment as more software suppliers step into the ring.

Linux helping small and big businesses

Every businessperson is always searching for technology bargains. Linux offers many ways for small-business owners to use it as an alternative to more expensive options.

Network Concierge allows a small-business operator to set up a Linux network server with a range of functions in such a way that even the computer-illiterate can master the product. The straightforward program enables you to take any personal computer, even an old 486 PC, and turn it into a file/print server for your network of Windows-based computers. You can then use this machine to make available printers or shared files, or to provide each network user with their own private file area. In addition, it will provide a Web server for internal or external use, as well as an email server. It will also let everyone on the network share access to a single Internet connection such as a cable modem, ADSL connection or other type of connection.

Network Concierge comes with a firewall to prevent outsiders from accessing your internal computer network. You set it up through a simple installation and administration program that is accessed through your Web browser, available for £68. Buy the same capability using products from Microsoft and others, and it will cost you much more.

The advantage of this product is its simplicity. Until now, installing and using Linux required an investment of time, as there is a learning curve. Network Concierge says anyone can set up it up within 15 minutes.

A subtle change in the marketplace has occurred in recent years, and Linux has become the tool of choice among many in the computing industry. Because of its flexibility, developers can take the core elements of Linux and put together innovative computer products such as Network Concierge. In addition to products like this, the emergence of many new 'network appliances' or specialised computer systems based on Linux, such as point-of-sale systems, fax servers and factory equipment controller systems, are being produced. The result is that entrepreneurs will see a lot of new, inexpensive and extremely functional products.

Network Concierge is at **www.nc4u.com** (Figure 6.19).

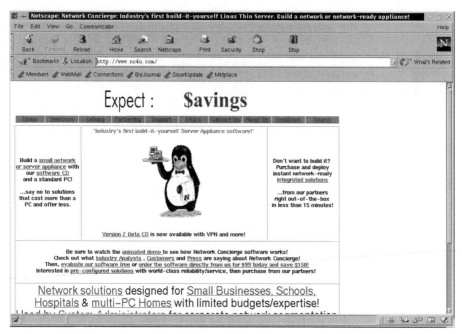

Figure 6.19   Network Concierge

Another example is SuSE's SALT cluster at **www.suse.de/en/hardware/ suse_hw/cluster/index.html** (Figure 6.20). This is a Beowulf cluster. Beowulf clusters are large arrays of Linux systems that together provide

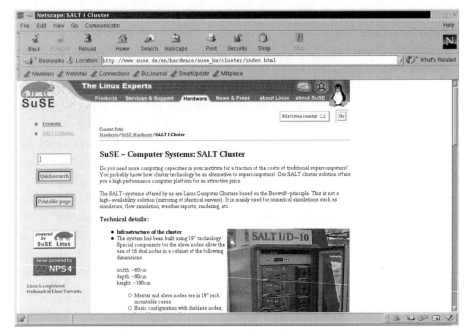

Figure 6.20 SuSE's salt cluster

similar computing power to established supercomputers for a fraction of their price. Linux Beowulf clusters are amongst the 500 fastest computers in the world. There is no limit to their speed. SuSE's SALT cluster is a cluster designed for corporate and scientific use.

Service and support

Linux service and support has become a big business, with large hardware manufacturers taking increasingly active roles in helping the open source community create software that is the best of its kind. IBM and Intel are now building Linux into their long-term e-business strategies; these giants are formulating ambitious projects that should establish Linux in the upper level of the corporate and research worlds.

Intel is preaching the gospel of compatibility, helping manufacturers prepare for migration to its IA-64 processor architecture upon the new chip's release later this year. The chip giant is working with all four major Linux distributors to make sure that they have working code when this chip is released. The company has the same sort of relationship with IBM, Compaq, SGI, Cygnus, and Hewlett-Packard, ensuring that their proprietary operating systems are ready for the IA-64; the fact that a young company like SuSE Linux finds itself in such exalted company is an indication of the importance of Linux to Intel. The effort, called the Trillian Project, has been under way for about a year. Intel has released the first work to the open source community, including a developer's release of a ported kernel and utilities, all of which will be distributed under the GNU Public Licence. The chipmaker has also made a substantial capital investment in SuSE Linux. For more information visit **www.intel.com/ebusiness/strategies/server/linux_sum.htm** (Figure 6.21).

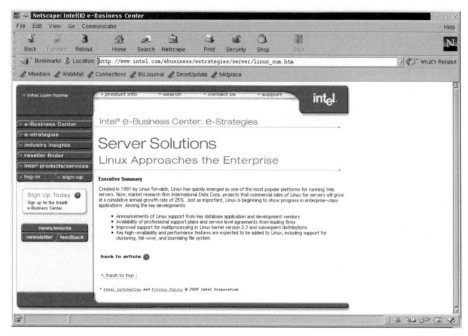

Figure 6.21   Linux and Intel

The support aspect

As the market for Linux server systems grows in the service provider community, universities and laboratories, so does the revenue that can potentially be derived from the servicing and support of those systems. Linux vendors and service companies, like SuSE Linux, can be reasonably sure that IBM will not put them out of business. There will be enough business for them to co-exist with the largest service organisations. SuSE Linux offers comprehensive support at **www.suse.de/en/support/index.html** (Figure 6.22).

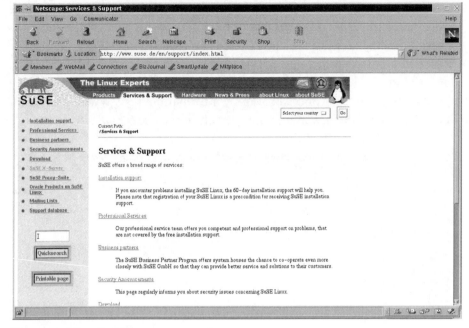

Figure 6.22 SuSE services and support

Many major organisations allow their business partners to support their shared customer base, and this arrangement works very well for all concerned. Having a global services organisation backing Linux can only broaden its acceptance as an enterprise-class operating system.

Training certification

At the end of the 1990s, most IT personnel would have been hard-pressed to find a basic Linux operating system course, and the concept of certification wasn't even discussed in Linux user groups. Today, Linux training and certification is a growing field, and the first classes of Linux-certified system and network administrators are taking home their certificates.

The main obstacle to Linux's gaining broad acceptance throughout companies is the lack of an industry-accepted certification process for Linux technicians, primarily system and network administrators. However, leading Linux vendors Red Hat and SuSE Linux and the Linux Professional Institute at **www.lpi.org** (Figure 6.23) have been encouraging the development of training courses.

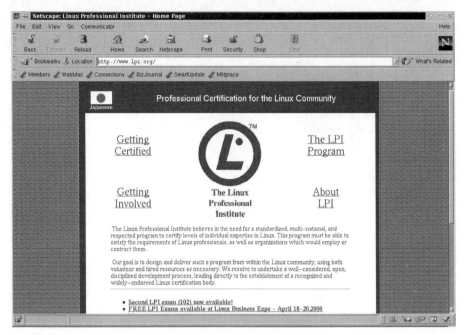

Figure 6.23 The Linux Professional Institute site

While the move to provide certification replicates the Microsoft and Novell models, the similarity ends there. Linux offers a real opportunity for development of vendor-neutral certification. The Linux Professional Institute's approach is to define distribution-neutral and vendor-neutral certification standards. Its multi-level program of exams – the first launched in late 1999 – is being administered through Virtual University Enterprise test centres. The Virtual University Enterprise Web site is at **www.vue.com/linux/** (Figure 6.24).

The Linux Professional Institute is supported primarily by contributions from business and individual sponsors, and its advisory council boasts not only major Linux and computing vendors and training providers, but even Novell, a Linux competitor. The easiest way to gain corporate, governmental and institutional support of Linux is to ensure that there is a bona fide support mechanism in place. Certification also provides industry recognition, an academic path for students and a mechanism for training centres and recruiting new Linux users.

The Linux Professional Institute is currently developing three levels of certification exams and is tabulating results of the first exam taken by 50 students in late 1999. The first level will feature three exams: a general Linux exam, an advanced exam, and an exam certifying specialisation in a specific distribution system. Levels 2 and 3, still in development, will offer advanced administration certification.

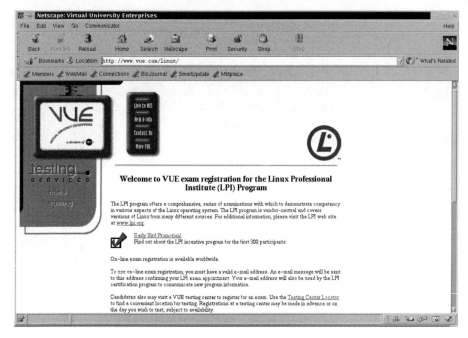

Figure 6.24   VUE exam registration at the LPI site

The Institute's certification will provide employers with a standard gauge to measure technical quality and competitiveness of a given candidate. The programme targets system and network administrators, job titles seen as 'high growth' for Linux support. When the Linux Institute revealed that certification exams were in development, 1900 interested students immediately registered for email notification of exam dates. When the first exam went live, 300 people registered for it within 48 hours. While the first wave of students appeared to be mostly UNIX programmers, today's Linux classes are a mix of professionals, causing trainers to move quickly to offer new courses.

Until now, Linux has been a cult, but now it is moving into the mainstream, which is where the need for training and certification comes in. As Linux gains in popularity and becomes more commercial, there is a growing need for training and certification. Clients are now asking for Linux training materials, but trainers are unavailable to provide them.

Linux supporters say the market for the operating system will continue to grow for several reasons: it is similar to UNIX, and it does not require as much administration as competing systems. Experienced UNIX programmers can expect to achieve Linux certification in about two to three months, half the time it would take to become a Microsoft network engineer or system administrator.

For businesses new to Linux, the logical first line of employees to be trained should be existing network administrators, and training should come before deployment. System administrators should be trained along with network administrators. While a Linux operating system may be less work to maintain in terms of network administration, companies should not be negligent in staff preparation. There is no need in small businesses for a dedicated Linux programmer. Unlike Windows, which requires constant reconfiguration and rebooting, Linux solutions require less maintenance.

Government and Linux

Proving that Linux is reaching established, mainstream and conservative organisation, an official team of the German Ministry of the Interior has released a statement which examines the possible use of open source software in the German administration. The statement concludes: 'Linux and FreeBSD and accompanying free or commercial software provide a stable, cheap, low-on-resources, safe and sufficiently supported environment even for professional offices.' The statement can be read in German at **http://linux.kbst.bund.de/ brief2-2000.html** (Figure 6.25).

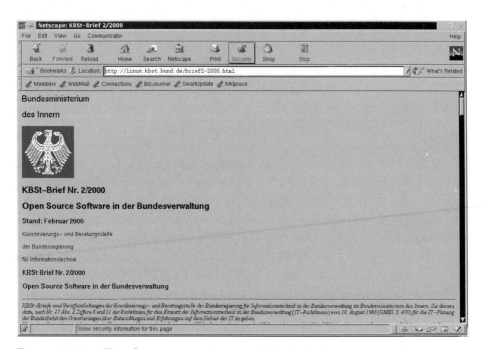

Figure 6.25   The German government's leaked open source document

There is also a computer-generated translation at **http://translator.go.com/ cb/trans_entry** (Figure 6.26).

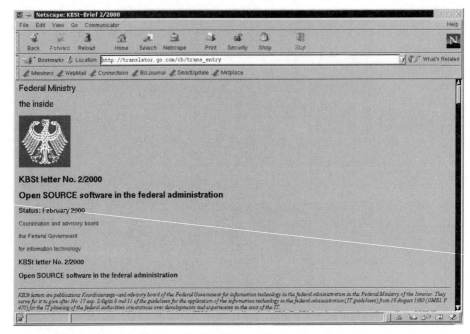

Figure 6.26 A translation of the open source document

The official site was eventually removed with an official note from the ministry saying it was only meant for 'internal use'; nonetheless it gives some insight into how governments are researching Linux.

NASA

The role of the phytoplankton in global climate change is currently not well understood. Learning more about this subject is very important in developing a better understanding of the carbon cycle and global climate, not from just a purely scientific view, but from a point of view that could impact the well-being of man and all other living things on Earth.

The NASA airborne oceanographic lidar (AOL) fluorosensor is a laser spectrofluorometer which is operated from an aircraft. By observing the laser stimulated fluorosence (LSF) and the colour of the ocean, NASA can measure levels of phytoplankton. These aircraft measurements greatly assist calibrating satellite ocean colour sensors, which can help estimate how much raw material they are taking up on a global scale and thus measure the primary productivity of the earth's oceans and seas.

The system that measures this consists of a rack-mounted 166MHz Pentium PC with 32Mb of RAM, and 4Gb of disk storage. The operating system on which all this runs is of course Linux. NASA engineers have written a detailed technical paper on the project, which includes block diagrams and functional descriptions of both the hardware and the software. This can be viewed at **http://lidar.wff.nasa.gov/aol-III.2/** (Figure 6.27).

Figure 6.27   Linux and NASA

Linux in schools

The Linux community has been extremely focused on getting Linux onto the desktop and into people's homes. Much work has been done in making Linux more user-friendly, more graphically-oriented, and easier to install and maintain. I consider this to be a good thing for the most part. However, the Linux community as a whole has ignored one major aspect of making Linux more popular, and that is getting it into schools and letting students work with it.

Today's educational market is dominated by Microsoft. Students begin learning MS Windows at an early age by working with it in schools. When they graduate and go on to buy their own computers, what will they buy? Most will buy what they are familiar with and that, of course, is a Windows box. In fact most will not even know that an alternative even exists. This is the same reason why software manufacturers offer amazing discounts on software to students and educators. As a student you can buy MS Office very cheaply. When you are no longer a student and need to upgrade, what will you buy? You will most likely buy what you are familiar with, and this time you have to pay the full price.

A problem with getting Linux into the hands of students is convincing the people who make the decisions that Linux is good and will help their students function in the real world. Most administrators think this means teaching students to use Windows and MS Office. Administrators believe that by teaching a student how to use a specific application that this helps them perform better later in life. Too many times I have seen so-called computer education classes as simple scripted classes where a student is simply led through the motions of pointing and clicking. We need to show administrators that this does not truly help a student, that we should teach a broader understanding of the concepts involved. If we can teach those concepts then students can apply them to a wide range of situations, applications and operating systems.

The one big advantage Linux has over Microsoft in the eyes of most school authorities is cost. Most school authorities are under pressure to get computers into their schools and get students using them. Most school authorities are underfunded anyway and this puts a lot of pressure on the individual budgets. If Linux could show school authorities that by spending the same amount of money they can buy more machines and as a result get computers in front of more students, then it would stand a chance.

First let us create a typical small school authority. This school authority has 15 schools in total with 750 teachers, an average of 50 per school. The authority has set a target of giving each teacher a personal workstation, two 30-station labs in each school, and three student workstations in each classroom. All the computers in the authority are networked together and fed into a central server. The authority would need a minimum of 3901 systems in order to meet this goal; the extra system is the server.

Let us look at the operating system and software costs involved of deploying all the workstations. Each workstation will have a minimum of the OS and an office suite installed on it. The typical cost for Windows NT/98 and MS Office for a school authority is around £100, cheap compared to what a normal user has to pay. So, for all 3900 workstations the OS and office suite would cost £403,450. Now, you have to calculate costs for the server OS and seat licences etc. The final costs are staggering, especially for small authorities that do not have large budgets in the first place.

Again, one of the advantages of Linux is that it is free. A real example of this took place last year, when the Mexican government embarked on an ambitious project to equip 140,000 schools with computers. The licence costs of Microsoft Windows were so high, even with volume discounts, that the Mexican government opted for Linux, saving an estimated £85 million. Over a large installed base, the cost advantage of Linux becomes compelling. All education institutions should take note.

Most school authorities hire consultants who tell them what hardware/software they need. Invariably this hardware is state of the art and expensive. The consultants tell them they really need this hardware, that if they don't get the latest and greatest hardware the students will fall behind in the technology race. Most administrators are under so much pressure to educate students about technology they believe this. Many do not realise that Linux does not need the latest and most powerful machines, and in most cases a Pentium 200 running on Linux will outperform a Pentium 500 running on Microsoft.

Obviously there would be costs after allowing for workstations for administrators, consultants, support personnel etc. I think you get the point, though MS tries to argue that the cost of deploying their OS is minimal. If the same school authority installed Linux along with StarOffice on the same workstations the total costs of the OS and office suite would be nil. With the money saved the school authority could have bought hundreds of other machines to put into the classrooms.

Students are generally offered computer programming courses. If a school authority wants to teach C/C++ as a language then they would probably need to buy compilers for the Windows machines. Of course, a C compiler is standard on all Linux systems and many free institutes of distance education exist for it. I also think that by teaching a student to program under a UNIX environment, it better prepares them to be able to program in the real world, especially at college/university. Most engineering schools use some flavour of UNIX as

Did you know that…?
UMSDOS
A special file system in Linux, which enables a UNIX-conform access (including long filenames and permissions) within a normal MS-DOS file system. This is somewhat slower than a 'normal' EXT2 file system, but is well-suited to demonstration purposes, as it does not need an extra partition.

the OS and a student who has learned to program and operate in Linux during their school years is far more prepared for engineering school in college.

One major drawback to Linux in the eyes of many people is that it does not have a lot of educational software. However, the list is growing all the time, and many people are hard at work on making the list longer. Hacking educational software is not seen as very glamorous. Kernel hacking, device drivers, GUI development and multimedia games seem to be what most people focus on.

SEUL, Simple End User Linux, is working on improving the use of Linux in education. If you are interested in Linux in education then check out the site and join the discussion list. The site details many of the current projects on and volunteers are welcomed. See **www.seul.org/edu/** (Figure 6.28).

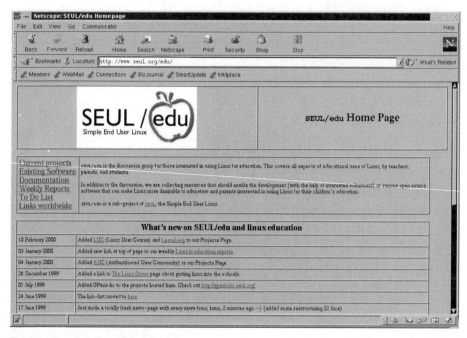

Figure 6.28 The SEUL site

The following sites are all committed to education.

SuSE have a site devoted to schools at **www.suse.de/uk/schools/index.html** (Figure 6.29).

There is an excellent FAQ at Open Source for Education: **www.ose.org.uk/ faq.php3?option=** (Figure 6.30).

Open Classroom is at **www.open-classroom.org/** (Figure 6.31).

I believe students should have a choice of the OS they are allowed to work on. Students need to be exposed to as much in the computing world as possible in their formative years so that they can make well-informed decisions when they finish their education and enter the real world.

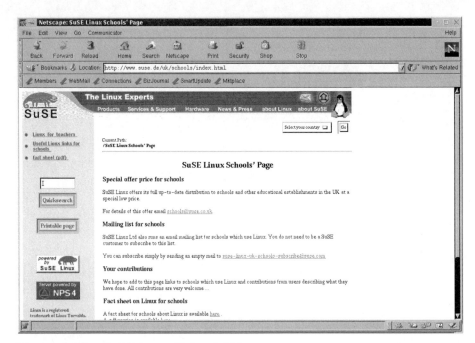

Figure 6.29 SuSE Linux Schools' Page

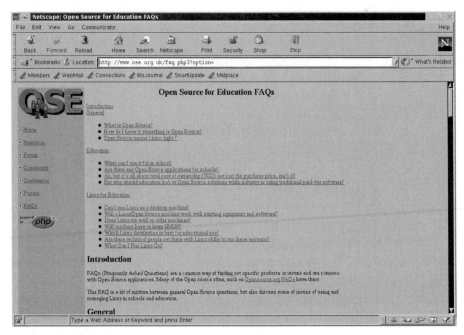

Figure 6.30 Open Source for Education FAQs

Figure 6.31   The Open Classroom site

Making money with Linux

The business world is confused when it comes to Linux. The current thinking is: how can money be made with a system that is given away? Similar things were said in 1993 when awareness started to build about the Internet. It did not fit into the style of a 'product' owned by a 'company'. Because of that, many executives believed it would be impossible to make money from it.

Today, few discount the economic impact of the Internet. It has been the incentive behind the creation of hundreds of thousands of business opportunities and tens of thousands of new companies. The US government recognises its massive impact, issuing a study that indicates the Internet is responsible for at least one-third of the economic growth enjoyed by the country in recent times.

Many people disregard Linux's potential to create wealth because it is free and is not owned by a person or company. The massive global adoption of Linux underway throughout many sectors of the high-technology community indicates that there is money to be made, yet Linux's philosophy remains intact.

So where is there money to be made? The stock market, eager to answer the question, has pushed up the price of Red Hat to an unrealistic and unsustainable height, and the shares of other companies involved with Linux have gained momentum in response. Although the development of user-friendly ver-

Although dozens of operating system vendors target their wares to embedded systems, the need to accommodate extremely tight hardware, software and cost constraints while meeting highly dedicated feature requirements often limits the practicality of using ready-made operating systems. For this reason, less than half of all embedded systems use commercial operating systems. Instead, the majority run on royalty-free software that has been custom-designed to precisely match system requirements and constraints.

However, this situation is changing, because embedded systems are rapidly becoming too sophisticated to be supported by home-grown operating system software, and due to the growing complexity of today's 32- and 64-bit microprocessors. It is changing as user-friendly graphical user interfaces and Internet connectivity weave their way into even the simplest intelligent devices. The idea of 'rolling your own' operating system is collapsing under the weight of time-to-market pressures, technology advances, and functionality expansion.

The embedded market is, therefore, in transition from a mostly roll-your-own to a mostly off-the-shelf operating system model. Microsoft has developed two operating systems to enter this growing market for outsourced embedded operating systems, Windows CE and Windows NT Embedded. Linux, now available in a broad spectrum of variations tuned to the diverse needs of the embedded market, is ready, willing and able to compete for its share of this market. A third option, made up of a legion of proprietary embedded operating systems each with unique features and benefits, is also vying for the opportunity to serve as the selected platform for embedded devices.

Under the assumption that the future belongs to mainstream standards, the choice boils down to two main options: Windows and Linux.

Why Linux will outclass Windows in the embedded market

Control

Embedded systems are about control. Controlling temperature. Controlling the user interface. Controlling resources. All these demand fine-tuning of the system's software to precisely match the needs of its users and its environment.

With commercial operating systems, your ability to adapt the OS to the needs of the particular application is limited. With Linux, you benefit from having a pre-existing operating system, including excellent tools, but with the freedom to shape and adapt the OS to match your application's exact requirements, since the source code is readily available to modify as you wish.

For example, one developer experienced in using both Windows CE and Linux described his frustration with Windows CE:

Windows isn't open source. Microsoft won't let you make modifications to the OS. Consequently, we're all dependent on Microsoft to provide feature enhancements and bug fixes. But given the diversity of the embedded market, it's impossible for one company (even Microsoft) to offer every feature that every embedded system requires. By contrast, if you need an unsupported feature in a Linux-based embedded system, you can simply add it. The embedded market doesn't need forced 'standardisation' on a single feature set. It needs diversity and the ability to innovate for a particular system's unique requirements.

The beauty of Linux is that it offers the benefits of a ready-made OS plus the flexibility of a roll-your-own approach.

Support

Embedded Linux has better support than Microsoft. The availability of source code means there are more experts to understand the problem, propose alternatives, and create solutions. The lack of this co-operative development model will leave Windows CE developers behind.

Although Microsoft has recently expressed a willingness to give developers access to their source code, that source is only made available for *reading* purposes and may not be used to alter the OS in any manner whatsoever, including fixing bugs.

Rapid innovation

The nature of the open source model is that Embedded Linux will evolve rapidly to meet the needs of the embedded community. Embedded Linux offers greater diversity, thus more opportunity, than Windows CE. The fact that there are hundreds of approaches to embedded Linux is a great way to ensure that at least one of them works. With an off-the-shelf commercial operating system such as Windows CE, if the one approach doesn't work, nothing works.

Linux is flexible

Linux is reaching a whole generation of new programmers, since Linux-based school projects are free from licence fees. This situation is reminiscent of Apple's penetration of the educational system through generous hardware and software donations in the late 1970s and early 1980s.

If you have tried to hire embedded system programmers recently, you are probably aware of the potential benefit of a strong 'magnet' like Linux in attracting talent.

The price is right

Embedded Linux pricing is infinitely flexible; you can pay as much or as little as you want for Embedded Linux. You can get as much or as little commercial support as you want. By contrast, with a Microsoft OS like Windows CE, there is structured pricing model that offers much less freedom to match your embedded system's precise requirements.

The cost benefit of Linux does not apply only to per-unit licence fees. It's also true of the development tools used by engineers to create the system. There are no special tools or expensive systems needed to create innovative and useful prototypes. You can find a broad spectrum of high-quality, readily available development tools, ranging from cost-free, open source tools to commercially licensed products from a wide range of specialists eager to assist with Embedded Linux system development, deployment and support.

It's about choice

Whenever embedded system developers select technologies and components, an overriding concern is the availability of alternate suppliers. Alternate source means reduced risk. As systems become more complex and challenging to support, it becomes harder to justify using sole-sourced components, whether hardware or software. In the past, there were no alternate sourced operating systems. Now, Linux has changed the rules; because it is open source, it offers an unlimited set of alternatives. In effect, open source is the ultimate alternate source. If you don't like your Linux distributor or development partner, you are free to pick another one. Or do it yourself. With Linux you are not locked into a single supplier, a situation that invariably results in increased costs to both you and your end customers.

The Internet

Linux is truly a child of the Internet. Open communication, made possible by the Internet, is a key factor driving the open source revolution. Linux might never have achieved the critical mass needed to achieve its current status as a mainstream operating system had it not been for the ease and flexibility of communications made possible by the Internet. On the other hand, the Internet has benefited greatly from Linux. Because Linux is a child of the Internet, the protocols and communications requirements needed to support the Internet are woven into the very fabric of Linux.

In short, Linux is connected. The Internet will certainly be a major factor propelling Linux into an increasing number of tomorrow's intelligent interconnected embedded devices. Consider the enormous variety of possibilities for such products, and you will start to see the huge market opportunity for Linux.

Reliability

We all expect embedded systems to keep running without operator intervention. Microsoft has not yet grasped the concept of reliability, offering 'three nines' (99.9 per cent uptime) on their Windows 2000 enterprise system to an industry accustomed to 'five nines' (99.999 per cent). Motorola recently cast its lot with Linux, announcing a High Availability Linux (HA Linux), a product they will target to the telephony and Internet equipment industries. Motorola says their HA Linux (on suitable hardware) will meet or exceed the 99.999 per cent uptime requirements of these reliability-intensive applications, which amounts to less than five minutes of downtime per year! The Motorola HA Linux site is **www.mcg.mot. com/cfm/templates/pressrelease.cfm?PageID=725** (Figure 6.32).

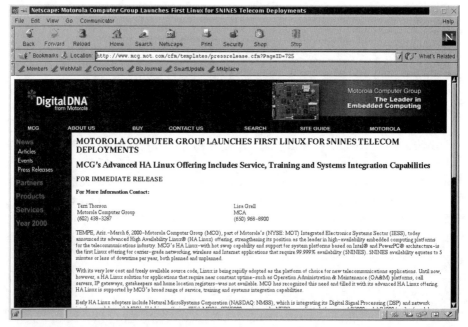

Figure 6.32   Linux and Motorola

While it is not hard to locate Linux-based servers that proudly proclaim how much time has transpired since their last reboot, this is not the case with Windows-based systems. How long has it been since your Windows system needed rebooting?

Flexibility

Unlike Windows, Linux is inherently modular and scalable. Linux can readily be scaled down into compact configurations barely larger than DOS, that fit on a single floppy. Conversely, Linux is well known as the server platform of choice, and is being designed into numerous Internet and telephony infrastructure programs. A growing number of projects even use Linux as the OS platform for multi-processor supercomputers. Since Linux source code is freely available, it is completely practical to customise the OS according to the specific requirements of your unique embedded system. Best of all, the enhancements and extensions to Linux that occur from these activities are generally returned to the open source code base pool for others to benefit from and evolve further.

It's not from Microsoft

Perhaps one of the main reasons Linux will be selected over Microsoft products is the strong undercurrent of anti-Microsoft sentiment among embedded system developers. Dr Peter Wurmsdobler of the Centre de Transfert des Microtechniques in France, offers a historical perspective on Microsoft's evolution from software enabler of the IBM PC, to where they are today: 'Microsoft democratised the computer market and served as a catalyst in making computers available to everybody. Later, however, they did as many revolutionaries do: they became dictators. History has taught us the inevitable fate of dictators.'

Conclusion

Microsoft is the most powerful software company in the world. They are obviously very proficient at a lot of what they do. They have been extremely successful in the personal and corporate computing space, and it is evident that they gain an advantage when they can focus their immense resources on what is essentially a single, very high-volume system architecture. Consider the market where Microsoft has been most successful: the desktop PC market. That market consists of some quarter of a billion PC-compatible computers (of various shapes and sizes) throughout the world, which share a common system architecture, common hardware components and common software components.

That sort of situation is attractive to Microsoft. On the other hand, the support-intensive embedded market, with its extreme diversity and fragmentation, represents a support headache for Microsoft and, by extension, for Microsoft's customers. This is probably why Microsoft has been unsuccessful in multiple attempts to penetrate the embedded market in the past. Who remembers Microsoft At Work, or Microsoft Modular Windows? And those are not the only abandoned efforts by Microsoft to establish a presence in the embedded market. A similar fate may well be lurking just around the corner for Microsoft's latest embedded offerings, Windows CE and Windows NT Embedded.

Rest assured, however, that Microsoft will aggressively pursue a handful of cherry-picked embedded opportunities that share characteristics such as these: user-interface intensive; serving as platforms for a multiplicity of application software; relaxed resource constraints; moderate (not high) performance requirements; quantities in the 10+ million units per year. What sort of embedded devices fit these criteria? A few obvious ones are set-top boxes, home entertainment systems and the automobile PC. Embedded device 'killer apps' like these will surely be the basis for some high-profile, hotly contested battles between Windows and Linux in the future.

However, in the extremely diverse embedded market consisting of tens of thousands of unique and highly specialised embedded device applications, home to more than 90 per cent of the world's annual production of microcomputer chips, Linux shows every indication of becoming the operating system platform of choice.

To find out more about Embedded Linux visit **www.linux-embedded.com/** (Figure 6.33).

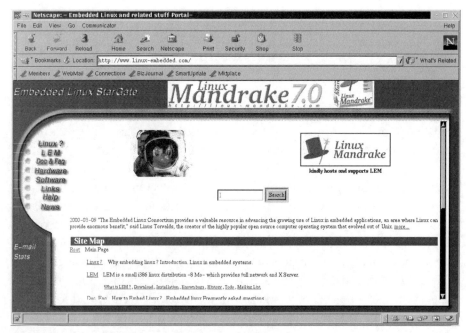

Figure 6.33   The site for Embedded Linux

7

Linux Information and how to find it

Searching for information on the Web ■

The first thing an inexperienced Linux user needs to do is to start reading about Linux. You may not be convinced yet that Linux is the OS for you. If that is the case, then going out and buying hundreds of pounds worth of books, which may all end up as a waste of money, is not a logical first step.

But we do have the eWorld. We all know that Linus Torvalds wrote the first Linux kernel, and that the current Linux version is 2.3, with 2.4 coming soon. So we should go to the source to get the definitive analysis on Linux. Well, not quite. On his Web site, Torvalds says, 'If you're looking for Linux information, you'll find more of it somewhere else, because I'm hopeless when it comes to documentation.' Check out **www.cs.helsinki.fi/~torvalds/** (Figure 7.1).

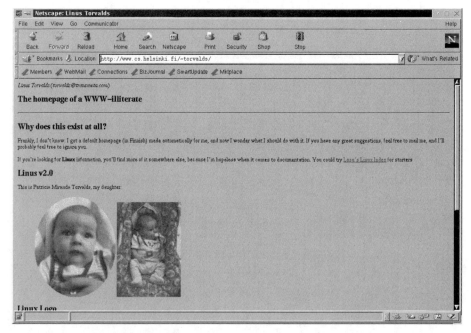

Figure 7.1 Linus Torvalds' Web site

Searching for information on the Web

Searching elsewhere for documentation and general Linux information I found thousands of Web sites, at least 370 UseNet news groups and more mailing lists than I care to count.

There are so many sites containing Linux information that you would end up with information overload. But for information for newcomers, and those who are just scratching the surface with Linux, it is difficult to find something appropriate. Most sites are geared toward those who have reached a certain level of familiarity with Linux, but newcomers who need to get their feet wet will have a lot of reading to do to find appropriate sites.

I do not claim to have made up a definitive list, or to have located the best Web sites for Linux beginners. I don't even claim to have looked at every relevant Web site so I'm sure I've missed some good ones. But I have been looking around and I can tell when information is pertinent or not. Here is a list of the sites I found useful to me, along with screenshots of their home pages. They are in no particular order.

The Linux Documentation Project is at **www.linuxdoc.org/** (Figure 7.2).

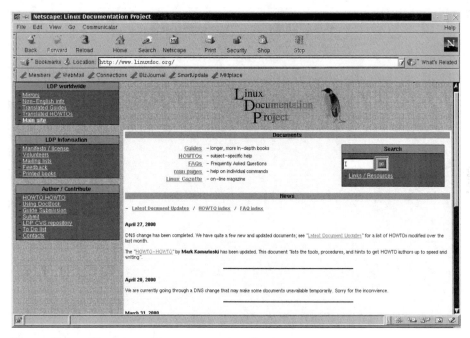

Figure 7.2   The Linux Documentation Project

As its name implies, this is a large project whose goal is to provide excellent documentation on Linux, for free, to anyone who wants it. There is a lot of information here but some of it is a little old. The volume and level of information can also be a bit much for a beginner. However, an experienced beginner, and those beyond the beginner stage, will find this site an excellent source that will be referred to repeatedly.

The Linux Ninja site (**www.LinuxNinja.com/index.php3**; Figure 7.3) has a document in progress called Linux Administration Made Easy (LAME), which addresses many issues relating to setting up and using Linux in a networking environment. While not exclusively geared to beginners, this document, which you can also download in other formats, contains a lot of material that will help to educate the beginner and familiarise him or her with Linux and its capabilities.

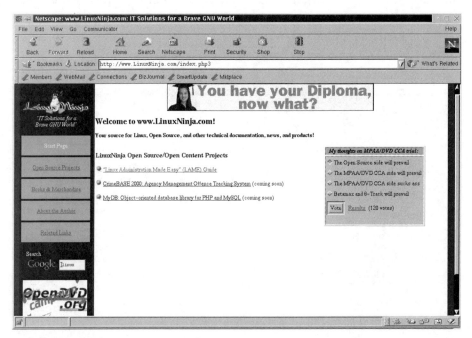

Figure 7.3 Download LAME from here

Linux Online (**www.linux.org/**; Figure 7.4) offers a Q&A format, which addresses a number of specific issues. Some of the questions are ones that raw beginners might have enough knowledge to ask. This is a more limited resource than some sites, which put enough information online to fill a book, but if you happen to be asking one of the questions it answers, then it is very helpful.

LinuxNewbie.org at **www.linuxnewbie.org/** is specifically for Linux newbies. It has articles written by Linux beginners who have discovered solutions to problems or questions, and who share their answers in an effort to help out other Linux beginners. The articles I read on this site were very helpful in aiding my understanding of Linux. This site also has a discussion group where Linux newbies can post their questions and problems, and others will help in finding solutions (Figure 7.5).

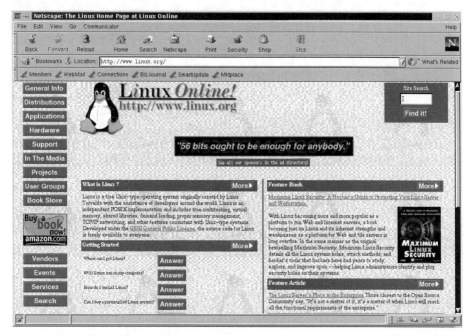

Figure 7.4 Find answers to your questions

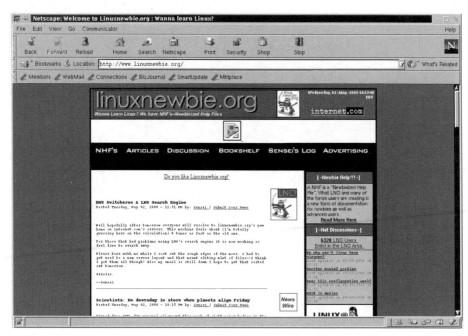

Figure 7.5 A site for Linux newbies

Tucows.com at **http://howto.tucows.com/LDP/HOWTO/Unix-Internet-Fundamentals-HOWTO.html** has a tutorial that features UNIX-like operating systems, which includes Linux, and gets right down to the most basic descriptions of how computers work and how the OS works on them, followed by a short description of the Internet and other information. If you want to follow the process from the hardware level upwards, this is a Web document that will probably fulfil your needs.

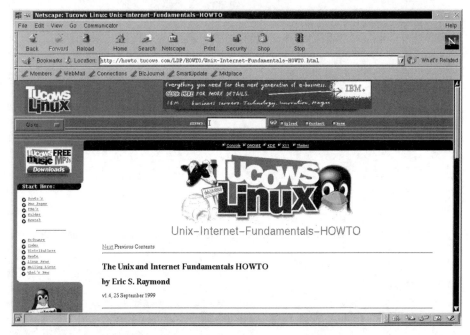

Figure 7.6   Read tutorials here

I recommend that you read several of these choices. There appears to be no single source that will completely educate the beginner. The large documents give a good grounding, and the specific questions can illuminate some areas that the larger documents fail to address. And of course, the Web changes minute by minute, so you should also look around for other resources that I may have missed, or those that are brand new.

Search engines

My favourite search engine for matters relating to Linux, and in fact for *all* searching, is Google, which provides a facility specifically for finding articles and references to Linux online. Google Linux Search is at **www.google.com/linux** (Figure 7.7).

Figure 7.7 The Google search engine

Software sites

Freshmeat is in some ways the backbone and nervous system of the Linux community. Every day between 10 and 30 new releases of software are introduced for Linux and other free UNIX systems, and Freshmeat covers virtually all of them. In addition, it also contains a searchable Appendix, a hierarchal listing of every release of every piece of software ever announced on Freshmeat. In addition, Freshmeat is often the site of original editorials concerning important Linux community issues. Visit Freshmeat at **http://Freshmeat.net/** (Figure 7.8).

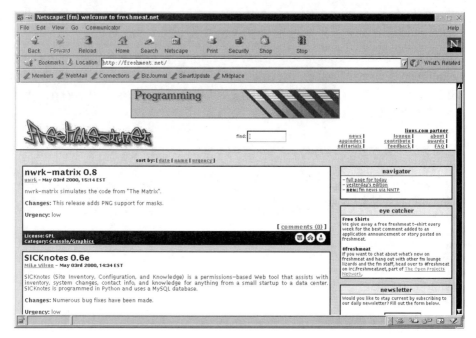

Figure 7.8 Freshmeat

Geared towards Linux newbies, **www.linuxberg.com** (Figure 7.9), from the creators of Tucows (The Ultimate Collection of Winsock Software), is a unique and useful Linux software Web site. Upon entering, the user is prompted to select from a list of approximately 146 mirrors from around the world, ensuring fast downloads to anywhere. This is especially convenient because, unlike Freshmeat where all you get are links to the applications' home pages, Linuxberg keeps a local copy of every piece of software they carry. In addition, each application is rated (a five-penguin rating is the best). Every Linuxberg server also houses copies of the most popular Linux distributions, downloadable for free.

As if this weren't enough, Linuxberg is also the home of the Linux HOWTO archive at **www.linux-howto.com**, which contains a searchable index of all the Linux HOWTOs and mini-HOWTOs.

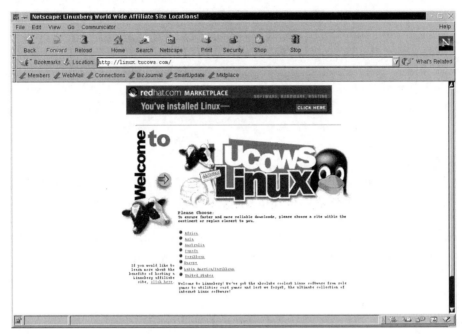

Figure 7.9   Linuxberg and Tucows

News

If Freshmeat is the nervous system of the Linux community, then Slashdot is definitely its mouthpiece; the site concentrates on technical and scientific articles as well as Linux stories. However, what really sets Slashdot apart from all other Web sites of its kind are the comments attached to each story. Anyone can log in and write a comment, which will instantly be posted to the site. If they wish, readers can comment on comments, resulting in long, tree-like discussions, which can continue ad infinitum (particularly sensational or interesting stories can easily collect 200 or more comments). This kind of interaction has made Slashdot a lively source of digitised information. Its greatest accomplishment is the 'Slashdot Effect,' which is what happens to Web servers with slow connections that inevitably crash after being linked into this site.

Slashdot sometimes draws criticism for its often wild discussions and quirky attitude; but whether you love it or hate it, there can be no doubting its impact on the Linux legions of the Internet.

There is a Slashdot clone for the UK at **www.linuxuk.co.uk** (Figure 7.10) and the main site is at **http://slashdot.org/** (Figure 7.11).

For total comprehensiveness, nothing can compare to **http://linuxtoday. com/index.html** for Linux news. Daily visits to this site will reveal listings of practically every mention of Linux in the mainstream press (both print and on the Web), and will provide up-to-date information on all important Linux happenings. This site is definitely a must for keeping up with the fast-changing world of Linux (Figure 7.12).

Another worthwhile news site is the Linux Weekly News (**www.lwn.net/**), which says it is 'Dedicated to keeping Linux users up-to-date, with concise news for all interests'. This site (Figure 7.13) boasts many original editorials, and is worth visiting for its informed opinions on Linux and open source.

Unlike the other news sites, **www.kernelnotes.org/** specialises in one thing: the Linux kernel and its frequent updates and additions. If you enjoy customising your kernel, then this is the site for you: it catalogues all the releases, providing a list of the major updates found in each one, as well as keeping track of the hard to find 'unofficial' patches. Look at the bottom of the page for useful links to documentation, distributions and more (Figure 7.14).

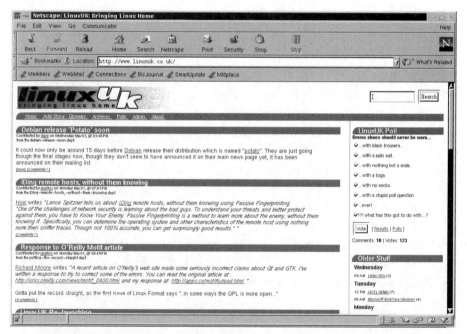

Figure 7.10   The UK clone site for Slashdot

Figure 7.11 Visit Slashdot for technical information

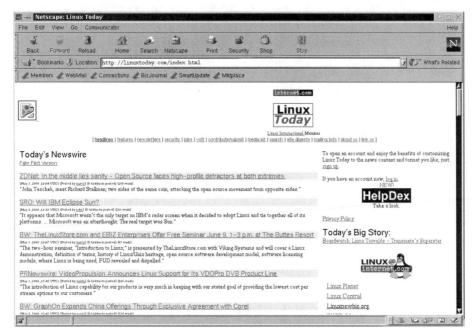

Figure 7.12 Up-to-date Linux news

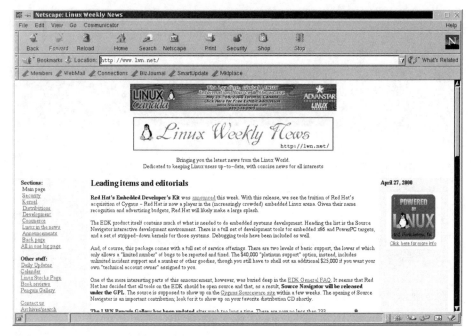

Figure 7.13   Linux Weekly News

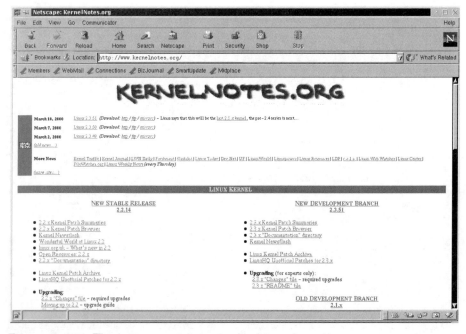

Figure 7.14   This site specialises in the Linux kernel

www.Linux.com (Figure 7.15) is the new 'catch-all' Linux site from VA Research, intended to be a useful all-round site, as well as a good place to get Linux information without using a search engine. This is good to visit for summaries of all the major aspects of Linux on the Web.

Figure 7.15 The new Linux site from VA Research

Themes.org at **www.themes.org** proves you can make a Linux Web site about anything. Themes.org is for true desktop warriors, who ditched Windows because it looked too bland. This site consists of collections of themes (sets of decorative images and colours) for various window managers (Afterstep, Blackbox, Enlightenment, FVWM, KWM, and Windowmaker to be precise), with a few other goodies thrown in. Check it out (Figure 7.16) if you want to explore Linux's configurability for the best possible look.

For general business news on Linux visit **http://linux.cnet.com/** (Figure 7.17).

Linux News at **www.zdnet.co.uk/news/specials/1998/10/linux_lounge/** is called the Linux Lounge and is well worth a visit (Figure 7.18).

Netproject is a site for end users who are working to achieve systems that enable e-commerce. Find it at **www.netproject.com/** (Figure 7.19).

UK Linux User Groups can be found at **www.lug.org.uk/** (Figure 7.20). These groups voluntarily help with the usage and set-up of Linux boxes.

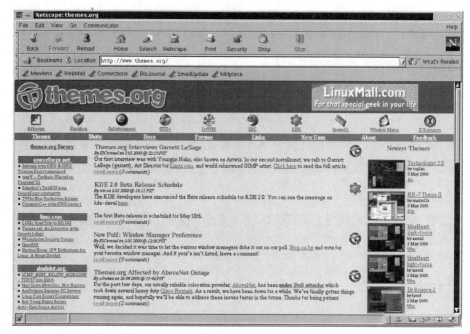

Figure 7.16   Change your Linux configuration

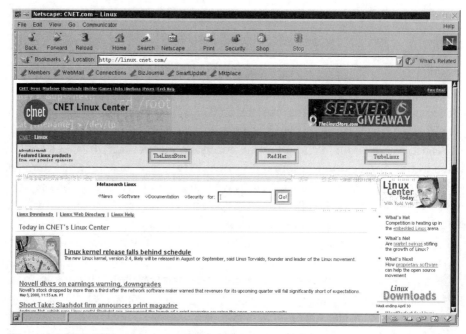

Figure 7.17   Business news on Linux

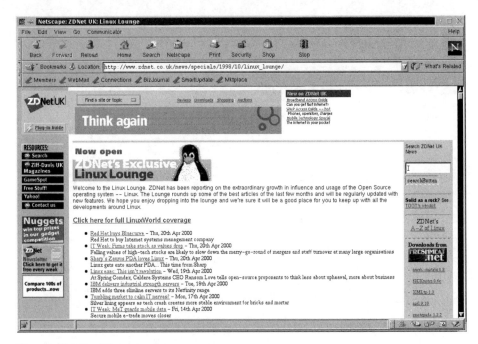

Figure 7.18 The Linux Lounge

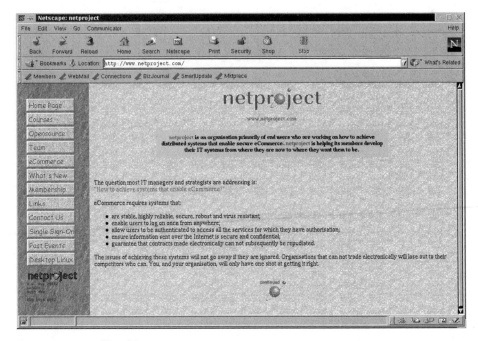

Figure 7.19 The Netproject site

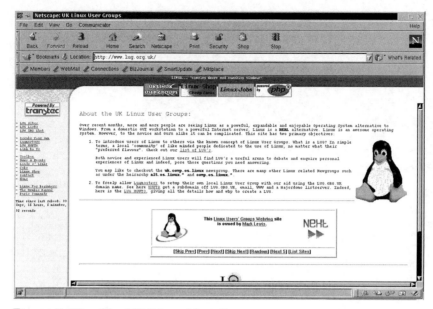

Figure 7.20 The UK Linux User Groups

Information on SuSE Linux

There is a very useful FAQ list for SuSE at **www.suse.de/en/linux/linux_faq/** (Figure 7.21).

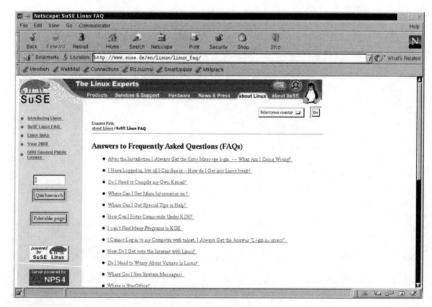

Figure 7.21 Find answers to FAQs here

For general information about SuSE/Linux then check out **www.fokus.gmd.
de/linux/linux-doc-faq.html** (Figure 7.22). This site is the best resource for
(generic) Linux FAQs and HOWTOs.

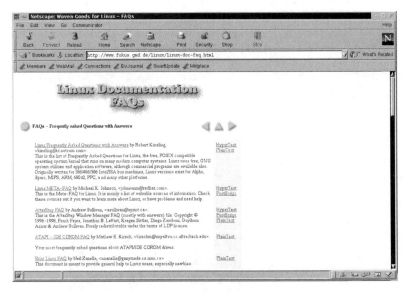

Figure 7.22   More answers to FAQs

Woven Goods for Linux is at **www.fokus.gmd.de/linux/** (Figure 7.23). This is
the first place I look if I am searching for a specific piece of information about
Linux. Do check out the software section, which is excellent.

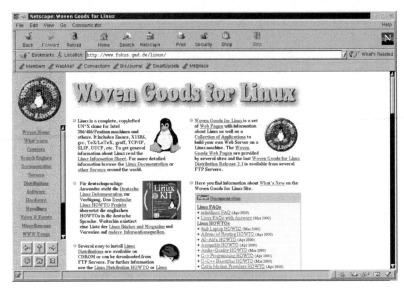

Figure 7.23   Look here for detailed Linux information

Games

Finally, Linux Games (**www.linuxgames.com/**) is a good site about games in Linux. As well as keeping you up-to-date on new titles from Id Software or Loki Entertainment, LinuxGames also hosts other game or game-related Web sites (Figure 7.24).

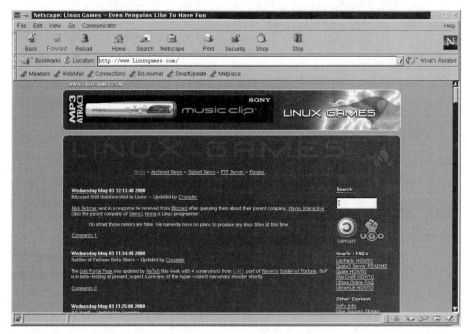

Figure 7.24 Find new Linux games here

The Future of Linux

Where is Linux today? ■

Where will Linux go in future? ■

The increasing influence of Linux ■

It is a very exciting time in the development and use of Linux. Its popularity and use is accelerating rapidly. But what is the future of Linux? Where does it go from here? And how does it get there?

Trying to make confident predictions about the future of Linux is a daunting subject. Things are changing so rapidly that most predictions become out of date within a few months, if not weeks or even days.

Imagine going back to a Linux users group meeting in late 1998 and trying to tell them what was going to happen over the next two years. You would have been laughed out of the room by even the most optimistic of the Linux advocates. I know from my own speaking experiences that in 1998 when I brought the subject of Linux into my presentations, nobody knew what I was talking about. Though in all fairness one of the few who understood Linux at that time was an IBM vice president who asked me what I thought of Linux. I replied in four words: "Linux is our future." He then took me into a room where many of his senior managers were assembled and, in front of them all, asked me the same question. I gave the same answer. Today I still reply in the same way.

Now try to look two years forward to 2002. Where will Linux and open source software be then? How will the Intel Itanium processor, the list 64-bit processor, and IA-64 technology change the fortunes of Linux? What will become of the commercial flavours of UNIX? Will the desktop environment of choice be KDE, GNOME, or something else? The honest answer is I have no idea.

We are in the middle of a revolution, the Internet revolution, of which Linux is just one aspect. The thing about revolutions is that nobody knows how they will turn out. We only know that things will be different afterwards. All you can do is stay alert and pay attention!

Every so often, a technology shift of unprecedented proportions comes along. The world economy, the high-tech industry and individual careers are changed by it. That is where we are today, with the explosive growth of and interest in Linux. Linux will devastate current high-tech business models, causing the most fundamental shift in the computing revolution since the arrival of the Internet. Yet Linux will provide unprecedented business opportunities to those who take advantage of what it offers; it is the Aladdin's cave of computing technology. The impact of Linux on high-tech share prices, margins, profits and costs will be massive, as completely new and different software standards takes hold. Companies will find it increasingly difficult to recruit and keep hold of the best in the high-tech field, unless they are willing to cater for Linux. Linux is more than a piece of software; it is a movement.

Shrink-wrapped games for Linux are now on the retail shelves. Maybe I should have seen this one coming, but, since I don't follow the games market, I missed it. The implications, however, are significant. The fact that profit-seeking enterprises realise that they can make money out of selling games for Linux destroys the myth that Linux is a server-only operating system.

For years, Linux has been a threat to Bill Gates and Microsoft. After the courtroom drama in the USA, which culminated with a proposal to force Gates to split the Microsoft empire into two, Linux could be about to send further tremors through the besieged Microsoft camp. The US court proposals may well bolster the rapid growth of Linux.

Where is Linux today?

The following points summarise Linux's position in the market today:

- It is a proven, efficient and highly stable operating system capable of running on desktop PCs as well as larger servers.

- It is an open source, publicly distributed system that encourages anyone or any company to enhance it and redistribute it without exorbitant licensing restrictions or fees.

- It is an architecture and user interface that is very similar to UNIX. Thus, a substantial community familiar with the UNIX/Linux model already exists within the IT industry.

- Linux is already widely deployed in some segments of the IT industry; it is a particularly popular OS for Internet servers.

- Linux is a relative 'newbie' in the desktop PC arena but it is getting much attention as an alternative to exsisting systems, particularly to Microsoft Windows.

Can Linux go further? The answer to this depends upon how attractive Linux is to the potential user community.

Linux's strength lies in its overall cost-effectiveness when compared to other OS alternatives. However, it has one weakness. While it is true that performance is always a major issue for applications that run on workstations, this is not always the case in the desktop arena. This arises from the simple fact that many current desktop applications perform well enough while using only a fraction of the hardware available from current top-end desktop PCs. The real weakness of Linux is not in performance, but in the availability of applications and support for the most commonly used devices, though this is changing daily.

Where will Linux go in future?

Linux will go only as far as its strengths and weakness will take it. Since its reputation is already accepted in the server community, it requires Linux to be accepted within the workstation and desktop communities.

Wider availability of applications and increased device support will also follow upon the heels of the increasing popularity of Linux. While the Linux community itself will continue to provide many important applications and enhancements, traditional software and hardware vendors will need to do their part by increasing support for Linux. Suppliers are more likely to do this as they begin to observe the increased popularity of Linux, as their customer base demands it.

This means that Linux will inevitably become vastly more popular in all of these areas. In the desktop arena especially, Linux could become a cost-effective and very popular alternative to Microsoft Windows. And if that happens, it will provide the industry with a solution to the Microsoft 'problem' which does not require government intervention or reverse marketplace engineering.

The increasing influence of Linux

Perhaps the most powerful movement in the software industry today is the continuing pace of Linux development, producing many reliable and successful applications. Linux is a seemingly impossible development methodology in which source code is developed and debugged not by one company or even one group of individuals but rather by a fragmented and distributed workforce simultaneously working toward a common goal. Believe it or not, these individuals are likely to have never met in person, and they provide most of their efforts on a volunteer basis. The only requirement of the open source movement is that source code must be freely distributed to customers and competitors alike.

Can distributed volunteer developers really produce reliable code? Can Linux further impact the software industry? How can business models exist if all the code is exposed for free? Could Linux influence my business? The answers to these questions may be surprising to you.

What's more, understanding the Linux movement may be important to all business executives, as the lessons learned may be applicable to every industry, particularly as we move toward an increasingly computerised economy. With that as a background, there are six things that every person should know about Linux and open source.

1. **Linux works.**

   It may seem unbelievable that volunteers can produce robust and complex software applications. Linux works, and it has an increasing base of users for all types of open source code, from operating systems to compilers to applications, to prove it. This movement, which began many years ago, thrives on leverage. By distributing a task across a large group of 'users', the project as a whole can move faster than if the project were controlled by a single entity. The most successful Linux software projects rely more on distributed testers and debuggers than developers, but the result is nonetheless remarkable.

2. **Linux development produces business-quality code.**

   The most obvious verification to the business success of Linux is the unwavering dominance of the Apache Web server. According to Netcraft, Apache runs on more than 60 per cent of the world's Web sites and has gained consistent market share. Linux supporters believe that distributed testing actually leads to more reliable code than could ever be achieved within a single organisation. Search the Internet for articles on Linux and you will find many users who believe open source code is, in fact, more reliable than Microsoft's Windows NT. And while Microsoft will vigorously disagree with this position, the fact that the argument exists at all is a testament to the obvious legitimacy of open source code.

3. **Linux business models are emerging.**

   Believe it or not, it turns out that you can make money off freely available software code. SuSE packages, distributes, supports and, more importantly, brands a version of the Linux OS. As with any software product, users value consistency and trust, and SuSE has done a wonderful job of packaging and distributing the Linux OS. Yes, you can download the code for free, but for many users, £35 is a reasonable fee for code that is easy to install, comes complete with documentation, and comes with the support guarantee of SuSE. Compaq, Oracle, Novell, IBM, Intel and Dell have all recently invested in Linux, and each company has entered into an agreement to either distribute or build upon the Linux OS.

4. **Linux is a tough competitor.**

   Competing with Linux can be compared to fighting an invisible opponent. For instance, Apache and KDE code is maintained by not-for-profit organisations. In addition, the software is available for free, which eliminates price as a competitive weapon. The pricing activities used by Microsoft to attack Netscape are less effective against an already free solution. And while Microsoft has begun to attack Linux, as well as the legitimacy of the open-source model, they have placed themselves in an awkward position by maintaining that the success of Linux is a competitive threat. As modifications of the Linux model thrive, more companies will be forced to adapt to this stable and reliable competitive force.

5. **Linux models are emerging for subject matter.**
   While the Linux elitist will disagree with the specifics of this comparison, we are seeing open source models emerge for subject matter in addition to software. Unquestionably, the most successful example is Netscape's Open Directory initiative. Once called NewHoo, this alternative directory listing to Yahoo! is built by an army of distributed volunteers, much in the same way that Apache and KDE is built by distributed programmers. In addition, the results of the directory are freely available on the Web for anyone to use, just as with open source code. Open Directory supporters argue that no one company's staff will be able to compete with its distributed volunteer base. In addition, the more sites that use the directory, the more volunteer editors will be drawn into the project. It is highly likely that the distributed open source content model will be replicated in other fields, and as with open source software, it may prove to be an agile competitor.

6. **Linux as a defensive weapon.**
   At the end of the day, Linux may prove to be more of a defensive weapon than an offensive one. Consider the example of Netscape's Open Directory project. By organising and freely distributing the directory data, Netscape may have neutralised the directory as a competitive differentiator for portal sites. We may, in fact, see more companies 'donate' certain intellectual property to the Linux community in an effort to diminish a particular aspect of competition.

As another example, it may be in America Online's best interests to make sure that Netscape's browser code is fully embraced and absorbed by the open-source movement. No single company is likely to challenge Microsoft's increasingly dominant market share in browsers; however, a freely available browser that can be customised by ISPs, software sellers and portals alike may gain popularity.

With the rising awareness of the potential for Microsoft to use the client as a control point for access to the Internet, a true open source browser initiative may be just what is required. Keep your eye on KDE's development of a browser.

Linux as a production model should be appreciated in the same light as Henry Ford's assembly line or a 'just-in-time' manufacturing process. By taking advantage of the electronic communication medium of the Internet as well as the distributed skills of its volunteers, the Linux community has uncovered a leveraged development methodology that is faster and produces more reliable code than traditional internal development. You can criticise it, doubt it, or ignore it, but you will not stop it. Linux is here to stay.

Part of Linux's magic is that it offers the computer-using community with a way to counterbalance Microsoft's dominance. There are many throughout the Linux community worldwide who are passionate in their belief that the future world of computing should not be controlled by one organisation. Consequently, tens of thousands of brilliant computer programmers are dedicating their time to Linux to ensure the world has an alternative.

The situation with Linux today is much the same as it was with the Internet in late 1993. Back then, the business world had first begun to hear of it and was coming to grips with the fact that something big was happening. The smart ones kept up-to-date with the Internet's emergence and discovered how to take advantage of it. It will be the same with Linux.

Well-established Linux users tend to be technically orientated people. The average Linux aficionado is likely to be more capable of dealing with technicalities than the average Windows user. As is evident by the trends of today, Linux software is going to become a lot easier to use, and the 'winners' in the application market are going to be those companies who have an established presence in the Linux world. In order to get that presence, you have to be the best of the best, because your critics are going to be extremely technically capable, likely to be more interested in the product than the marketing. Just make the best product available, and the people who appreciate that will recommend the best product forever. In writing this I have no reservations in recommending SuSE Linux. I have experimented with many Linux distributions, and all of them are good, but I always come back to SuSE. I feel that they dot the is and cross the ts. SuSE Linux is a complete, comprehensive Linux distribution with an excellent range of bundled commercial software and good support for useful hardware add-ons like ISDN and sound cards. If you want a good all-round package that you need no experience to be able to use, then SuSE Linux is for you.

As they say at SuSE Linux – have a lot of fun!

Appendix I

SuSE Linux Frequently Asked Questions (FAQs)

After the installation I always get the error message login: — what am I doing wrong?

You are not doing anything wrong. The installation is complete and you may log in to the computer with your user name and password; initially, only the 'root' user exists.

I have logged in, but all I can see is earth:# — how do I get into Linux itself?

You are already in Linux. You probably want to start the graphical user interface (GUI). This needs to be configured first (with SaX, for example). Then you can start the graphical system (X Window System) with the command `startx`.

I use my computer on my own, so why do I always need to log in?

Linux is a multi-user system. In order for Linux to know who is working on it, you need to specify a user name and password. Incidentally, you should only work as user 'root' if you need to make changes to the system (installing and configuring software and so on). For normal operation you should create a standard user, then you cannot do any damage to the system itself.

Do I need to compile my own kernel?

No, in most cases this is definitely not necessary. The kernel has now become so large that there are some 800 options which need to be considered in the configuration! Since it is impossible to keep track of all these different configurations, I strongly recommend inexperienced users not to recompile the kernel. If you still want to do this, you do so at your own risk, and SuSE cannot provide any installation support if you compile your own kernel.

Do I need to compile the kernel for sound support?

Not since kernel 2.2.x.

Where can I get more information on SuSE Linux?

For information on SuSE Linux, use the handbook. Documentation on the programs can be found in `/usr/doc/` packages, introductions in the HOWTOs in `/usr/doc/howto/de` for German, and in `/usr/doc/ howto/en` for the English HOWTOs. They can be read, for example, with `less/usr/doc/howto/en/DOS-to-Linux-HOWTO.txt.gz`. In KDE you can also read the files (even though they are compressed) with the command `kedit`.

Where can I get special tips or help?

You will find the SuSE support database at **http://sdb.suse.de/sdb/en/html/index.html**. Enter a search phrase or browse through the History link of the SDB.

How can I enter commands in KDE?

Click on `K,Tools`, then `Terminal`. Alternatively you can press Alt+F2 and then enter xterm. Then you will have a 'Terminal' (often mistakenly referred to as the DOS-window), in which you can enter commands.

I can't find many programs in KDE.

You can start all programs from a terminal window (xterm) by entering the program name and pressing Return/Enter.

I cannot log in to my computer with telnet. I always get the answer `Login incorrect`.

You are probably trying to log in as user 'root'. For security reasons this is not possible via telnet. With YaST, set up a normal user account; you can log in with this username. Then you can change to the user root with su. It is much better and safer, however, to use the program ssh instead of telnet; the ssh program uses encoded, and thus secure, connections. You can find this program in the sec series.

Do I need to worry about viruses in Linux?

No. In Linux there are no critical viruses to speak of. Also, viruses cannot cause any significant damage to the system as long as they are not invoked as root. The only virus scanners which exist in Linux are for searching mail for Windows viruses (if Linux is being used as a router).

Where can I see system messages?

As 'root', enter the following command in a terminal window: `earth:#` `tail-f/var/log/messages`. Other programs of interest in this respect are: top, procinfo and xosview. Messages which are sent at boot time can be seen with the command `earth: # dmesg` or with `earth: # cat/var/log/boot.msg`.

Where is StarOffice?

You will find StarOffice as the package so_en, which can be found in the series pay. Use the SuSE installation program YaST to install it, which will then tell you which CD you need to insert.

I have found a bug in SuSE Linux. Where can I report this?

First, make sure it really is an error in the program, and not just an operating or configuration problem. You should also first read the documentation in `/usr/doc/packages` and `/usr/doc/howto`. It is possible that the error has already been detected, and information on this can be found at Linux's support database at **http://sdb.suse.de/sdb/en/html/index.html**. Enter a search pattern, or step through the History link of the SDB, to see if the problem has been registered. If it appears not to have been documented, send a description by email to **feedback@suse.de**, quoting your registration code.

How can I access my CD?

You must first mount the CD.

I cannot remove my CD from the drive: what should I do?

You must first unmount (`umount`) the CD.

How can I see the space I have available in Linux?

Use the command `df-h`.

Can I 'cut and paste' in Linux?

Yes. If you want to use 'cut and paste' in text mode, the program gpm must be running. The rule for both the X Window System and in text mode is highlight by pressing the left mouse button, and drag and insert with the middle mouse button. The right mouse button has a special function in many programs.

How can I install programs?

Programs on the SuSE Linux CDs are best installed with YaST. Note that many of the larger programs can be found in the series pay.

I have a program 'only' in source code. How can I install it?

For many programs you need a certain amount of know-how. In short, unpack the archive with the command `tar xvzf name.tar.gz`, read the file INSTALL or README and follow the instructions. Usually this entails `a /configure; make; make install`. Please note that no installation support will be given for self-compiled kernels.

I need firewall, masquerading, mailserver and WWW server software. Can I get help for these from Installation Support?

No. SuSE Installation Support is to help you to get Linux up and running. For topics which go beyond installation support, there are some good books available, as well as excellent documentation in `/usr/doc/packages` and `/usr/doc/howto/en/NET3-HOWTO.txt.gz`.

Is my hardware supported?

Look at **http://cdb.suse.de/cdb_english.html** to find out. Also, the command `less/usr/doc/howto/en/Hardware-HOWTO.gz` will provide you with additional information.

How can I defragment my hard drive?

Linux has an intelligent file system. This filesystem makes defragmenting superfluous, because hardly any fragments occur in the first place. You should just make sure that your partitions do not become more than 90 per cent full (using the command `df-h`).

I have read something about partitioning: what is this?

Partitioning means the splitting of the hard drive into individual subsections. SuSE recommend using SuSE Linux with at least three partitions (one for boot files, one for Linux itself, and a swap partition).

Do I need to delete Windows in order to be able to use Linux?

No. But Linux does need enough free space on the hard drive. Run the program defrag in Windows, then run the program fips on the first SuSE Linux CD, in the directory `\dosutils\fips\fips20`. With this program you can resize Windows partitions to create more space for Linux. Back up your files first!

How much disk space do I need to install Linux?

You will get by with about 380Mb, but SuSE recommends approximately 1Gb. If you want to install everything, you will need over 4Gb.

I would like to remove Linux; how do I do this?

Delete the Linux partitions with the command `fdisk`; you may need to run the Linux version of fdisk. Then you should boot from the MS-DOS floppy disk and enter the command `fdisk/mbr` in DOS or Windows.

In YaST the menu item 'base network configuration' cannot be selected.

During the installation you specified that you would like to run the computer as a DHCP client. In this case, the network configuration is performed by the DHCP server. If you do not want this (this is the standard case), start YaST, and in the `network configuration/DHCP Client` menu select `No`. Then you can return to the `Base network configuration` menu.

My computer doesn't seem to react any more. Can I just press the reset button, without worrying?

If your computer no longer reacts to the mouse or keyboard, this does not necessarily mean that the entire computer has crashed. A single program may have blocked the mouse and keyboard, and other programs may continue to run normally. If the computer is accessible from outside (serial terminal, network), you can login, and close the program causing the trouble with `killall`. If you do not have this option you can try, using `Ctrl+Alt+F2,` to switch to a different console, and to end the process which is stuck from there. If the computer does not react to any key input, wait until there has been no hard drive activity for at least 10 seconds, and then press the reset button.

What is a mirror? Why shouldn't I just download things from `ftp.suse.com`?

Since there are many users downloading from the server at the same time, it would soon become overloaded. For this reason there are a number of ftp servers containing a mirror-image of the SuSE server. Such servers are therefore referred to as mirrors. You should choose the server nearest in physical location (i.e. in your own country) to facilitate faster download times. A list of such mirrors is available at **http://www.suse.de/en/support/download/ftp/index.html**.

What sort of directories are /var, /etc, /bin and so on?

The /var and /etc directories contain important system configuration files and /bin contains the commands needed to start the system.

How can I display, edit, move, copy or delete files?

You can either use the standard Linux shell tools, or you can use the program mc in a text console (a clone of a well-known DOS/Windows tool). On the desktop (in X Windows mode) you need to open a terminal, using Alt+F2; enter xterm; then type mc.

I cannot find any .exe files. Where have all the programs gone?

In Linux, executable files normally have no file extensions. Most programs are located in /usr/bin and /usr/X11R6/bin.

Appendix II

General Linux Frequently Asked Questions (FAQs)

Does Linux run on Windows?

NO. Linux and Windows are both operating systems. An operating system is a group of programs that control your computer and allow you (and other programs) to interact with it. You can only run one operating system at a time (although more than one operating system can be installed on the same computer). You either interact with your computer through Linux, or you interact with it through Windows.

Will my Windows programs run on Linux?

The bad news: Probably not. Linux was designed to be compatible with UNIX, a powerful operating system designed for multi-user, multi-tasking environments. Windows is not designed to be compatible with UNIX. In general, a program designed for Linux or another UNIX-like operating system will run on Linux just fine. Because the internal structure of Windows is so different, it takes considerable effort to 'port' applications from Windows to UNIX-like systems.

The good news: There are many applications available that are designed for Linux, so whatever applications you used under Windows, you can probably find something similar that runs on Linux, and the chances are you will be able to download it *for free*. Many companies publish software that runs on both Windows and Linux, notably Netscape, Corel WordPerfect and StarOffice, a cross-platform office suite that will make Windows users feel right at home. There is also a project called WINE whose goal is to build Windows application support on top of Linux and other UNIX-like systems. The project is still under development and may not be suitable for all users, but it has reported many successes running Windows programs on Linux using its software. Learn more at WINE headquarters at **www.winehq.com/**.

Will Linux run on my hardware?

If you have an off-the-shelf PC, the answer is probably yes. You can check the Linux Hardware Compatibility HOWTO at **http://metalab.unc.edu/LDP/ HOWTO/Hardware-HOWTO.html** to find out for certain.

Can I have Windows and Linux on the same computer?

Yes, in fact this is very common. It is referred to as a *dual boot* configuration. It's not difficult to set up a PC this way, but you must be careful not to lose any data in the process.

Where can I get Linux?

Linux can be purchased on CD-ROM in retail computer stores or from online vendors, or you can download the whole operating system directly from the Internet. You can get a list of Linux distributors and links to their Web sites by reading the Distribution HOWTO at **http://metalab.unc.edu/LDP/ HOWTO/Distribution-HOWTO.html** or Obtaining Your Copy of SuSE Linux at **www.suse.com**.

How do I set up hard drive partitions for Linux without deleting Windows?

Normally, you will need to resize your existing Windows partition in order to make room for Linux partitions. Each Linux distribution comes with a utility called FIPS that can do this job. Details on using FIPS can be found at the FIPS home page: **www.igd.fhg. de/~aschaefe/fips/**. For more detailed information see the Partition Mini-HOWTO at **metalab.unc.edu/LDP/ HOWTO/mini/Partition.html**.

How do I edit text files?

Like so many Linux questions, this one has many answers. The two classic Linux text editors are emacs and vi. Both are available on virtually any Linux installation, though if one is missing it is more likely to be emacs due to its larger size. Both are well documented, which is good because neither is very intuitive in my opinion. For users coming from a Windows world, I would recommend a program called joe, a clone of the old WordStar program. It's not as simple as DOS Edit or Notepad, but it has the advantage that you can display the help hints while you type, which makes it extremely easy for beginners. There is also an editor called pico that is easy to use and is available on most UNIX systems since it is included in the pine email package. If you have KDE (**www.kde.org**) installed, kedit is by far the easiest text editor to use. It is basically an incarnation of Notepad, with similar limitations and ease of use, albeit with a few extensions.

Tips

How do I log in?

On the console, see **http://sdb.suse.de/sdb/en/html/cep_login.html**. See also the section in the manual. In the graphical login screen enter your username or click on the icon for a specific user. Hit Return. Enter the password, and then hit Return again. Note that the password will not be shown in a readable form while you enter it.

What Linux training is available?

See **www.lpi.org**. This presents generic training for a variety of different Linux vendors, with a generic part and modules for each distribution.

Which application replaces those I am currently running?

Microsoft Office is replaced by StarOffice (free), ApplixWare (roughly £70), KOffice (beta quality), WordPerfect (usually only the word processor function). Visual Basic is replaced by Basic implementations. No real VB clone exists. There is an attempt to write a VB Virtual Machine for Linux; see **http:// SoftworksLtd.com/**. A converter to Java can be found at **http:// 207.126. 104.133/products/converter.asp**.

Internet Explorer is replaced by Netscape Navigator. For email software, use Netscape mail or pine (in a shell). There is a multitude of other mailers on SuSE Linux as well.

For other software see **www.fokus.gmd.de/linux/linux-softw.html**.

How do I install a new package?

See the corresponding chapter in the SuSE manual for a complete description. Put one of the SuSE CDs into the drive. Start YaST by clicking on the YaST icon under X or by entering 'yast' in a root-shell. Go to `Choose/Install` packages/Change/Create configuration/ `Name of a soft-ware series`, for example, 'fun'. Choose a package (e.g. 'freeciv') by highlighting the selection with the cursor keys, then hitting Return. Press F10 twice. Choose `Start Installation`. If additional packages are needed, YaST will warn you. In this case choose 'Auto', then `Continue`. The package will then be installed. YaST will prompt you for the correct CD(s). When finished, press ESC to go back to the main YaST screen or go to Main menu. SuSEconfig will run and configure your system, and the package is then ready to use. Exit YaST by hitting ESC.

Is my hardware supported?

See **http://cdb.suse.de/cdb_english.html** and **www.fokus.gmd.de/linux/ linux-hardware.html**. If you are looking for first-hand experience on using the hardware, search on **www.searchlinux.com**.

Why should I use any other user than root?

The root user can easily destroy the whole system. It is the only one with sufficient permissions to erase every single file in the system. While working as root in order to administer the system there is nothing to be afraid of, but working under that account daily is dangerous. You might accidentally erase an important file. Therefore work under another account, for example, one that was created during the installation. The system then will not let you erase anything other than your own files.

How do I access a data CD-Rom?

Put the CD-ROM into the drive. If you are using KDE, left-click on the CD icon on the desktop. The CD-ROM will then be mounted, that is, it can be accessed as part of your normal file system. You can also mount a CD-ROM by executing the command 'mount /cdrom' in a root-shell.

The CD drive cannot be opened. What do I do?

This usually means that there is a CD in the drive which is either being used right now (music CD) or which is monted in your file system. Unmount it, either by executing the command `umount/cdrom` as root in a shell or by right-clicking on the CD-ROM icon on the KDE desktop and choosing the `unmount` option. If the system doesn't let you unmount the CD, this means that you are still accessing the CD somewhere. This can be by either an application or a file manager that points to the CD-ROM drive. Also, when you have changed in a shell to the directory where the CD is mounted, it will not be possible to unmount the CD and to open the drive. Change to a directory independent of the CD, then try to unmount the drive again.

How can I hear a music CD?

There is an icon on the KDE desktop that starts the kscd CD player. Note that the soundcard must be configured in order to listen to CDs. See the description in the manual for how to configure a soundcard.

How do I access a floppy disk?

On the KDE desktop, left-click on the floppy icon. In order to unmount it, either enter the command `umount/floppy` in a root shell or right-click on the floppy icon and choose `unmount`. Do *not* remove a floppy disk from the drive while it is still mounted. This can damage the content of the disk! There are also mformat, mcopy, mdir and mdel tools which let you communicate with the floppy drive from the command line as you could under DOS systems.

Why do I have to shut down the system before I switch off the computer?

Linux is a UNIX system. It always keeps some information stored in the file system in memory in order to allow faster access to it. This speeds up the system considerably. As a consequence, the information about the disk content which is in memory does not necessarily fit the information that can be found on the physical disk. This information is only updated every few seconds. Switching the machine off prevents an update of the information on the disk. This is the main reason why a UNIX system has to be shut down. There are further reasons; all programs running in the system should be terminated prior to switching the system off. This again has to do with the risk of losing data. The reason why you may not remove a floppy from the drive prior to unmounting it is very similar. Most operating systems have to be shut down for the same reason before you may switch off the machine.

Can I access my Windows partition?

Yes, you can. FAT and FAT32 partitions can be accessed by both reading from and writing to it. Windows NT file system partitions should be accessed in read-only mode only.

Glossary

Acronym

Quite often abbreviations are called acronyms. FTP, ASCII and GNU are well-known acronyms.

Alias

This expression is often used in connection with the *shell*. An alias is a short cut to commands with long names, or frequently used ones.

API

Java application programming interface.

Argument

Functions and routines are passed as arguments to process.

ARP

Address resolution protocol. Used to translate Internet protocol (IP) addresses into physical hardware addresses.

ASCII

American Standard Code for Information Interchange. Each letter of the alphabet is represented by an 8-bit code. ASCII is most often used to store written characters.

BeOS

Be Operating System.

Bit

A single bit of data that represents either 1 or 0 (on or off) in binary code.

Bottom-half handler

Handlers for work queued within the kernel.

BSD

Berkeley Software Design.

Byte

Eight bits of data.

C

A high-level programming language. Most of the Linux kernel is written in C.

CISC

Complex instruction set computer. The opposite of *RISC*, this is a processor which supports a large number of often complex assembly instructions. The X86 architecture is a CISC architecture.

CPU

Central processing unit, the main engine of the computer. See also *micro-processor* and *processor*.

CRT

Cathode-ray tube (used for certain types of monitor).

CUI

Centre Universitaire d'Informatique of the University of Geneva.

Data structure

This is a set of data in memory comprised of fields.

Device

In Linux devices are accessed via special entries in the file system, which are located in `/dev/`. These entries contain the device numbers with which the kernel can reach the device drivers.

Device driver

The software controlling a particular device; for example, the NCR 810 device driver controls the NCR 810 SCSI device.

DMA

Direct memory access.

DNS

Domain name system.

DRAM

Dynamic random access memory.

Editor

Editors are programs for changing text (for example, by entering text). Well-known Linux editors are GNU Emacs and the UNIX editor vi.

EIDE

Extended *IDE*.

ELF

Executable and linkable format. This object file format designed by the UNIX System Laboratories is now firmly established as the most commonly used format in Linux.

Ethernet

Widely-used network hardware for *LANs*. It has a bus structure. Its speed was originally 10Mb through coaxial cable, but today networks are usually made up of twisted-pair cable at speeds of up to 100Mb.

Executable image

A structured file containing machine instructions and data. This file can be loaded into a process's virtual memory and executed. See also *program*.

EXT2

Second Extended File System. EXT2 is the native file system used by Linux. It offers a high throughput, long file names, permissions and error tolerance.

FTP

File transfer protocol is a means under UNIX for transferring files from one machine to another. On one side is the FTP server (the machine sending the files), and on the other, the FTP client (the receiver of the files).

Function

A piece of software that performs an action. For example, returning the bigger of two numbers.

GNU

GNU stands for 'GNU is not Unix' and is a product of the Free Software Foundation (FSF) whose aim is to provide a completely free (source code available at no cost) UNIX-compatible operating system. In this process, all UNIX tools are completely rewritten and new functionality is added. Linux benefits from these tools but should not be confused with GNU.

GPL

General public licence.

HTML

Hypertext markup language.

IDE

Integrated disk electronics.

Image

See *executable image*.

Inode

The EXT2 file system uses inodes for organising information on files. Inodes contain information such as the owner of its file, permissions and so on.

Interface

A standard way of calling routines and passing data structures. For example, the interface between two layers of code might be expressed in terms of routines that pass and return a particular data structure. Linux's VFS is a good example of an interface.

IP

Internet protocol.

IP address

A numerical 32-bit Internet address, usually in decimal notation as four sets of numbers separated by dots (for example, 192.168.10.1), which are uniquely assigned to a machine connected to the network. If a machine contains several network connections (gateways), it will also have several IP addresses.

IPC

Interprocess communication.

IPO

Initial public offering.

IRQ

Interrupt request queue.

ISA

Industry standard architecture. This is a standard, although now rather dated, data bus interface for system components such as floppy disk drivers.

ISP

Internet service provider. A firm or person providing Internet services.

Kernel module

A dynamically loaded kernel function such as a file system or a device driver.

Kilobyte

A thousand bytes of data, often written as Kbyte or Kb.

LAN

Local area network. This usually means that it is small and generally super-vised by one system administrator. LANs are frequently connected to other LANs via a gateway, combining to form a *WAN*.

Language

Computer-readable language, written in binary code, such as C, C+ and Pascal.

LCD

Liquid crystal display (another type of monitor).

LISP

LISt processing.

Main memory
This is often referred to as RAM, or random access memory. RAM access is very fast in comparison to hard drive access. On Linux, this memory is often referred to as physical memory.

Manpages
Traditionally the documentation for UNIX systems lies in manpages, which can be read with the command man.

Megabyte
A million bytes of data, often written as Mbyte or Mb.

Microprocessor
An integrated CPU. Most modern CPUs are *microprocessors*.

MIME
Multi-purpose Internet mail extensions. These were originally intended to expand electronic mail options (for example, to add sounds or images), but the technology can be used for many other things.

Module
A file containing *CPU* instructions in the form of either assembly language instructions or a high-level language such as C.

Mount point
The directory where a partition or another device is attached to the Linux file system.

Mounting
This describes the 'mounting' of file systems into the directory tree of the system. As a rule, an empty directory serves as the *mount point*.

Object file
A file containing machine code and data that has not yet been linked with other object files or libraries to become an *executable image*.

ODBC
Open database connectivity (ODBC) is a widely accepted application programming interface (API) for database access.

OEM
Original equipment manufacturer.

OS
Operating system; also open source.

Page

Physical memory is divided up into equally sized pages.

PCI

Peripheral component interconnect. A standard describing how the peripheral components of a computer system may be connected together.

PCMCIA

Personal Computer Memory Card International Association.

Peripheral

An intelligent processor that carries out work on behalf of the system's *CPU*; for example, an *IDE* controller chip.

Pointer

A location in memory that contains the address of another location in memory.

POSIX

Portable Operating System Interface is a set of standard operating system interfaces based on the UNIX operating system.

Process

A *program* or executable file in action. Often, it is referred to as a task.

Processor

Short for *microprocessor*, equivalent to CPU.

Program

A coherent set of *CPU* instructions that performs a task, such as printing 'hello world'. See also *executable image*.

Protocol

A protocol is a networking *language* used to transfer application data between two co-operating processes or network layers.

RAD

Retail application developer.

RAID

Redundant array of inexpensive disks.

RAM

Random access memory; physical memory of limited capacity, which can be accessed for read and write purposes at a relatively high speed. See also *ROM*.

Register

A location within a chip, used to store information or instructions.

Register file

The set of registers in a processor.

RISC

Reduced instruction set computer. The opposite of *CISC*, RISC is a processor with a small number of assembly instructions, each of which performs simple operations. The ARM and Alpha processors are both RISC architectures.

ROM

Read-only memory. A CD is a good example of ROM.

Routine

Similar to a function except that, strictly speaking, routines do not return values.

rpm

From SuSE Linux 5.0, rpm package manager is the standard. With rpm, software packages can be installed and uninstalled, and queries can be made to the database.

RSA

RSA is a public-key cryptosystem developed by MIT professors Ronald L. Rivest, Adi Shamir, and Leonard M. Adleman in 1977 in an effort to help ensure Internet security.

SCSI

Small computer systems interface.

SGML

Standard generalised markup language.

Shell

This is a program which acts as an interface between the operating system and a human user. Also called a *command shell*, the most commonly used shell in Linux is the bash shell.

SMP

Symmetrical multi-processing. This occurs in systems with more than one processor which share the work fairly amongst those processors.

Socket
A socket represents one end of a network connection. Linux supports the BSD socket interface.

Software
CPU instructions (both assembler and high-level languages such as C) and data. Mostly interchangable with *program*.

SQL
Structured query language.

System V
A variant of UNIX produced in 1983.

Task queue
A mechanism for deferring work in the Linux kernel.

TCP
Transmission control protocol.

Telnet
An Internet software application, Telnet creates a connection to a (remote) host and gives you a login to this machine, provided you have an account.

UDMA
Ultra direct memory access.

UDP
User datagram protocol.

URL
Uniform resource locator. The term for the addresses of *HTML* pages in the World Wide Web.

Virtual memory
A hardware and software mechanism for making the physical memory in a system appear larger than it actually is.

WABI
Windows application binary interface.

WAN
Wide area network. Unlike a *LAN*, this network connects computers that are located over a wide area.

WIMP

Window, icon, menu, pointing device (or pull-down menu).

XML

Extended markup language.

Index

future of Linux 190–5
fvwm95 39

Gameboy 46
games 46, 109–11
  information sources 188
General Public Licence (GPL) 9–10, 119
German government 155–6
Gerstner, Lou 143
GhostScript 112–13, 121
GIMP 34, 43, 44, 134 1
'glue-in' distributions 28
GNOME 36–7, 121, 134
GNU project 9, 58, 119, 121–2, 124
  GNU emacs 42, 121
  GNU HURD 121
  GNU troff 78, 79
  Gnumeric 50
goals of Linux 60, 64–5
Google Linux Search 177
governments
  and Internet regulation xvii
  use of Linux 155–6
GPI, (General Public Licence) 9–10, 119
graphics 43–4
  debugging tool 41
  LaTeX-graphics 42
Great Internet Worm 86
groff 78
GUI (graphical user interface) 9, 17, 30–1,
  37, 83

HA Linux 168
Halloween documents 118
HALT instruction 105
hangs/crashes 101, 105
  reset 105, 200
hard disks 53–4
  defragmenting 199
  exchangeable 100
  partitioning 100, 199, 202, 205
  space requirements 199
hard links 178
hardware 2–3, 10, 50–4, 199, 202, 204
  information sources 51
  performance 18, 22–3
  for VMware 99
help *see* support
Heretic II 110, 111
Hewlett-Packard 139
High Availability Linux (HA Linux) 168
history of Linux 7–11

Hohndel, Dirk H. 126
home directory 33

IBM 138, 143–7, 147, 150
  Netfinity servers 104, 144, 145–6
  Project Monterey 144
  ThinkPad 100, 103
image editing 34
importing Word documents 79–80
information sources 172–88
  Freshmeat 177–8
  games 188
  Google Linux Search 177
  hardware 51
  LAME (Linux Administration Made Easy)
    174
  Linux Documentation Project 173
  Linux HOW TO 179
  Linux Lounge 183, 185
  Linux Ninja site 174
  Linux Online 174
  Linux Weekly News 180, 182
  Linuxberg 178–9
  Linux.com 183
  LinuxNewbie 174, 175
  Linuxtoday 180
  Netproject 183, 185
  news sites 179–86
  search engines 177
  Slashdot 179–81
  software information sites 177–9
  SuSE Linux 186–7
  Themes.org 183
  tucows.com 176, 179
  User Groups 183, 186
  Woven Goods for Linux 187
Informix 70
Ingres 70
installation 21, 49, 50–1, 129
  base Linux 115
  disk space requirements 199
  Network Concierge 148–9
  preinstalled systems 129, 140
  of software 49, 198–9, 203–4
  support 17
  of VMware 99
  YaST2 installation tool 21
  see also, hardware
Intel 150–1
lintent logs 18
interfaces *see* user interfaces

MkLinux 106, 107
Mockapetris, Paul 133
modems 53, 102, 103
modules 55
monarchy Web site 25–6
monitors 54
Monterey Project 144
Motif 70
    CD-Player 45
    OSF-Motif 41
Motorola 168
Mozilla Licence 119
mpegplay 43
MS-DOS 3, 4
    emulator 45–6, 89–92
    licence 46
multi-tasking 24, 29, 105
MWave technology 103

NASA 156–7
Nessus 87
Netatalk 113
Netfinity servers 104, 144, 145–6
Netproject 183, 185
Netscape 11, 33, 61, 105, 122, 147
    Mozilla project 119, 130
    Open Directory 194
Netware 147
Network Concierge 148–9
Network File System (NFS) 88
networks 23
    remote login 39
    security 40
    Virtual Private Network (VPN) 96–7
    Window Manager 38–9
    new technology 61–2
NewHoo 194
news sites 179–86
Nintendo 46

object code 6
office applications 65–78
    Applixware 42, 66, 69–71
    Corel Office 2000 66
    databases 70
    KOffice 66, 71–3, 79–80
    LaTeX2e 42, 66, 76–8
    LyX 42, 65–6, 76–8
    Maxwell 66
    SIAG Office 66, 74–5
    spreadsheets 66

StarOffice 42, 50, 66–8, 198
TeX 42, 65, 66, 76–8
WingZ 66
word processors 42, 66, 75–80, 202–3
WordPerfect 34, 42, 66, 75–6
Open Classroom 160, 162
Open Directory 194
Open Source for Education 160, 161
open source group 122–3
open source software xviii, 11~15, 58,
        117–19
    Apache 41, 82, 105, 123, 130–1, 193
    BIND (Berkeley Internet Name Domain) 133
    GIMP 34, 43, 44, 134
    GNOME 36–7, 121, 134
    K Desktop Environment (KDE) 36–7, 71,
        79–80, 134
    Mars 147
    Netscape Mozilla project 119, 130
    Perl (Practical Extraction and Report
        Language) 12, 131
    SAMBA 113, 134, 147
    Sendmail 12, 86, 123, 132–3
    squid 40, 134
    WINE 45, 89–90, 96, 134
    also see applications; office applications;
        software
OpenGL 41
operating systems 3–5, 23
    closed operating systems xviii
    in the embedded systems market 164–5
    multi-tasking 24, 29
    UNIX systems 5–6, 7, 24, 28–9, 78, 120
Oracle 70, 138, 143
ORB (Object Request Broker) 72
OSF-Motif 41

package formats 26–7
package managers 49
Palmisano, Sam 143
Partition Magic 100
partitioning hard disks 100, 199, 202, 205
PCMCIA slots 103
performance of hardware 18, 22–3
Perl (Practical Extraction and Report
        Language) 12, 131
phytoplankton 156
'Ping of Death' 11, 85
port scanners 84
position in the market 127, 137, 142, 191
PostScript 112–13

Accompanying CD-ROM
SuSE Linux 7.0

SuSE Linux 7.0 installation

Important

Please note that the evaluation CD is released without support. Sources of information are available on the internet in electronic form, in the handbook, from the SuSE Support Database, as well as the SuSE Linux mailing lists.

Requirements

You can set up SuSE Linux on your computer from the evaluation CD without having to change the partitioning of the hard drive. If you have approximately 100 MB (ideally, 200 MB) of free space available on your hard drive, the evaluation system can even be installed permanently.

A computer with at least the following hardware is required: Pentium processor (or compatible), 64 MB RAM (memory), a bootable CD-ROM drive and a BIOS supporting 2,88 MB boot images, as well as a partitioned and formatted hard drive.

Installation with YaST2

Please note: Be sure to make a back-up copy of your data before the installation. There are no guarantees that data will not be lost. If you're careful the chances can be drastically reduced, although not completely. You should therefore make a back up before the installation!

1. Insert the CD and start up the computer. After a few seconds Linux will begin to load. If the computer does not boot from the CD you'll probably need to change the boot-order in the BIOS.

2. An automatic hardware detection is carried out. After the automatic hardware detection, the installation routine tries to create an approx-

imately 100 MB working file (**suselive.usr**) but if you have less than 128 MB RAM, a swap file for virtual memory (**suselive.swp**). The actual configuration data of the system is stored in the file **suselive.640** when the system is shut down. As a rule, these files are stored on the first FAT partition (drive C:). The CD is mounted.

3. You can determine the basic settings with the help of the graphic installation program, YaST2; language, keyboard, and time-zone. The mouse is automatically detected in most cases. Detailed texts on the left-hand side provide context-related help.

4. The user and root logins need to be given passwords.

5. You have a chance to adjust the standard resolution (1024 × 768 is recommended) and the colour depth (16 bpp is recommended) and then to adjust the monitor; for this, select the »Test« button.

    If difficulties arise here, try to abort the configuration with Ctrl-Alt- Backspace; if all else fails, switch the computer off, to prevent hardware being damaged. You can try the installation again by entering at the boot prompt, right at the beginning: **linux vga=3**.

6. With YaST2 you can configure the »printer«, »sound«, »Internet access« and »network«. If you want to leave these items out, select »Complete Installation« straight away.

7. The installed system is started.

8. You can log in via the KDM (KDE Display Manager) and use the programs in the KDE graphical interface (K Desktop Environment).

Caution

You should never just switch the computer off. Always shut down the computer properly. To do this, end the running KDE session with »Logout« and in the KDE dialog, again with »Logout«.

Booting SuSE Linux and working with the system

If the files to store the system data can be set up on your hard drive, SuSE Linux 7.0 can be started as often as you want. Boot the computer each time with the evaluation CD and just wait until the KDM login-dialog appears.

Important: since all programs are loaded directly from the CD, you may not remove the CD from the drive during operation. It lies in the nature of things that the overall system, for this reason, runs quite a bit slower than if SuSE Linux were installed on the hard drive, and would use its own file system. The speed is dependent on the CD-ROM drive used – 'fast' drives take more time!

More information

The complete handbook for SuSE Linux:

ftp://ftp.suse.com/pub/suse/i386/6.4/docu/book-de.pdf

The SuSE Linux mailing lists:

http://www/en/support/mailinglists/

If you have questions, please check the SuSE Support Database:

http://sdb.suse.de

More information on SuSE Linux can be found in the Internet at:

http://www.suse.de

No warranty

As this CD is licensed free of charge, there is no warranty for the program, to the extent permitted by applicable law. Except when otherwise stated in writing the copyright holders and/or other parties provide the program 'as is' without warranty and liability of any kind, either expressed or implied, including, but not limited to, the implied warranties of merchantability and fitness for a particular purpose. The entire risk as to the quality and performance of the program is with you. Should the program prove defective, you assume the cost of all necessary servicing, repair or correction.

In no event unless required by applicable law or agreed to in writing will any copyright holder, or any other party who may modify and or redistribute the program as permitted in the licence, be liable to you for damages arising out of the use or inability to use the program (including but not limited to loss of data or data being rendered inaccurate or losses sustained by you or third parties or a failure of the program to operate with any other programs), even if such holder or other party has been advised of the possibilities of such damage.